Alan Ellis

THE FEDERAL SENTENCING GUIDEBOOK:
A PRIMER FOR ATTORNEYS, DEFENDANTS, FAMILY AND FRIENDS

ALAN ELLIS

JAMES H. FELDMAN, JR.

LAW OFFICES OF ALAN ELLIS
495 MILLER AVENUE
MILL VALLEY, CA 94941
415-380-2550
FAX: 415-380-2555
E-MAIL: AELaw1@aol.com

http://www.alanellis.com

Publisher's Cataloging in Publication Data

1. The Federal Sentencing Guidebook
2. Alan Ellis
3. James H. Feldman, Jr.

Library of Congress Catalog Card Number 2007943617
ISBN 0-9664436-5-9

CONTENTS

Chapter 1

Federal Sentencing Under the Advisory Guidelines

From Mandatory to Advisory Guidelines

A newspaper might report that a defendant convicted in federal court on 20 counts of mail fraud and ten counts of money laundering faces 600 years in prison. Such a report would contain a grain of truth. The mail fraud statute in most cases has a 20-year maximum sentence.[1] Money laundering has a 20-year maximum sentence.[2] If the defendant received the maximum sentence on each count, and if each sentence was run consecutively, he could receive 600 years. But the news story would not begin to inform the public of how federal sentencing really works. It would not tell what that defendant realistically faces.

Twenty years ago, prior to the Sentencing Guidelines, stories like that made a little more sense. Back then, with a few exceptions, a federal judge could sentence a convicted defendant anywhere from probation to the statutory maximum. All that changed when the Sentencing Guidelines went into effect in 1987. The Guidelines were part of a major overhaul of federal sentencing called the Sentencing Reform Act (the "SRA").

The SRA was supposed to correct some unfair aspects of the old system. Under the system before 1987, there were often unexplained differences between one person's sentence and another's. People who committed the same offense under similar circumstances could receive very different sentences for no apparent reason. White collar defendants often received minimal terms of imprisonment or probation, no matter how serious the case. Some politicians thought this was too lenient. In some parts of the country, African-American defendants often received harsher sentences than white defendants who committed the same offense conduct. Some politicians hoped a guideline system would correct this injustice. Under the old system, it was impossible to tell at the time of sentencing just how much of a prison term a defendant would actually serve. Even though many defendants received what seemed to be long sentences, most were eligible for parole after serving one third of their sentences and some even less. Even then, the actual parole date was unpredictable.

The SRA tried to solve these problems by creating a nearly-mandatory guideline system. Under that system, a sentencing court would use the guidelines to determine a sentencing "range" — 51-63 months, for example. A court was generally required to sentence a defendant somewhere in that range. Lower sentences were possible if the defendant could show a mitigating factor that the guidelines did not adequately consider. These were called "downward departures." Upward departures were also possible if the government could prove the existence of aggravating factors that the guidelines had not adequately considered.

While the mandatory guideline system "solved" some of the things Congress thought were "problems" with the old sentencing system, it created others. Unfair sentencing disparities still existed. Some disparities were caused by the way the guidelines rewarded defendants who "cooperated" with prosecutors. "Cooperation" means helping the government investigate or prosecute other people's crimes. Cooperators often received lower sentences than the people they helped convict, even when the cooperators' offense conduct was more serious. No matter what other mitigating circumstances existed, none counted as much as "cooperation."

A prosecutor's decision of what charges to bring could also create unfair differences in sentences. For example, two defendants who committed identical frauds could receive vastly different guideline sentences. If the prosecution charged one defendant with money laundering and fraud, and the other one only with fraud, the defendant convicted of money laundering would have a higher guideline range. This would happen even if the two of them actually did the same illegal acts.

White collar defendants no longer received lenient sentences. That "problem" was "solved" by imposing unfairly long sentences on most white collar defendants. Sentences in almost every kind of case became longer under the guidelines. The longest and most unfair sentences of all were often imposed in drug cases. This was true even when there was no violence, or where a particular defendant's involvement was relatively minor.

Even though the mandatory guideline system "solved" some "problems," it had a fatal flaw — it was unconstitutional. Unfortunately, it took nearly 18 years for the Supreme Court to recognize this defect. On January 12, 2005, the Supreme Court ruled in *United States v. Booker*[3] that the mandatory guideline system was unconstitutional in that it violated the Fifth and Sixth Amendments. The Supreme Court's reasoning went like this: Under the Sentencing Reform Act's mandatory guidelines system, the maximum sentence a defendant could receive depended on the guideline offense level. The offense level depended on the facts of the case — such as a quantity of drugs or money. The Constitution requires any fact that increases a maximum sentence to be charged in an indictment and proved to a jury beyond a reasonable doubt (or admitted by the defendant at a guilty plea hearing). But under the mandatory guidelines system, facts that determined the offense level (and therefore the maximum sentence in most cases) were generally not charged in an indictment. They were determined by the sentencing judge by a preponderance of the evidence — not by a jury beyond a reasonable doubt. A "preponderance of the evidence" simply means "more likely than not."

The Supreme Court perhaps could have solved this problem by requiring guideline facts to be charged in indictments and proved beyond a reasonable doubt to juries. But it did not. Instead, the Court focused on the parts of the Sentencing Reform Act that gave rise to the constitutional problem. It removed the language from the SRA that required judges to sentence within the guideline range in most cases.

In some ways, sentencing did not change much after *Booker*. Sentencing facts are still not charged in indictments. Sentencing judges still calculate a defendant's guideline offense level and criminal history score. And they still decide the facts necessary to make these calculations by a preponderance of the evidence. What is different is that sentences are not controlled by the guidelines in the same way they used to be. Judges have more flexibility to evaluate cases individually.

Now that the guidelines are no longer mandatory, the most important part of the SRA is the requirement that the sentencing judge impose the sentence that is "sufficient, but not greater than necessary,"[4] to fulfill the purposes of sentencing as defined in the statute. In other words, the court must impose the lowest sentence that still meets these goals. What are those goals? Promoting respect for law, just punishment, deterrence, protection of the public, and rehabilitation and treatment of the defendant.[5]

To determine the lowest sentence that meets these goals, the remaining parts of the Sentencing Reform Act require a court to "consider" seven general factors: two of those factors are the sentencing range suggested by the guidelines and the guideline policy statements.[6] The five other factors a court must "consider" are: (1) the facts concerning the defendant and the offense,[7] (2) the purposes of sentencing,[8] (3) the "kinds of sentences available,"[9] (4) the need to avoid sentences that are unnecessarily higher or lower than those in similar cases,"[10], and (5) the "need to provide restitution to any victims."[11]

The sentencing guideline range is only one of seven factors a court must "consider" before it imposes sentence. But often judges treat it as the most important. Many courts still impose most sentences within the guideline range in most cases. But even for courts that are more willing to impose sentences outside that range, the guidelines are still important. They are the starting point for considering a lower or higher sentence. It is therefore still important for defendants to have a basic understanding of how the guidelines work. Prior to trial, defendants need to understand how the guidelines might apply to their cases. This understanding can help them evaluate plea offers proposed by the prosecutor. It can also help them explore the possibilities of working out pleas. To evaluate a plea offer, defendants must be able to compare the likely guideline range under the offer to the likely range after an unsuccessful trial. They must also be able to take into account the likely range after an "open plea." An "open plea" is a guilty plea to all counts without a plea agreement.

While technical treatises — generally hundreds of pages long — have been written to help lawyers understand the guidelines, until the Law Offices of Alan Ellis published the first edition of this Sentencing Guidebook in 2003, there was no resource designed to help the occasional Federal Practitioner, their clients families and friends. We wrote this booklet back then to fill that gap. Over the past four years, it has helped clients and their families understand the guidelines.[12] It has also helped them communicate with their lawyers. When clients have a basic understanding of the guidelines, it is easier for their lawyers to help them make informed decisions about their cases. While the 2003 Guide remained useful after *Booker*, many of its assumptions were no longer true. We have updated it to reflect the way that federal sentencing now works. We have also updated the Practice Tips chapter and included a reprint of one of Alan Ellis' federal sentencing columns from *Criminal Justice*, the journal of the Criminal Justice Section of the American Bar Association. The column explains our approach to federal sentencing after *Booker*. We have also included a feature article we wrote for *Criminal Justice* entitled "Litigating in a Post-Booker World" and one from the *Champion*, the monthly magazine of the National Association of Criminal Defense Lawyers (NACDL) on white collar sentencing after

Booker. Finally, we have added a soon to be published article entitled "Tips on Getting Your Client into The Best Prision Possible."

What this booklet will *not* do is to help someone estimate a guideline range in a particular case or to formulate an argument for a lower sentence. Sentencing law is constantly changing. Only by working with an attorney who keeps up with these changes can a defendant get the information he needs to make important decisions about his case.

The Advisory Guidelines

An overview of the guidelines

When the guidelines are applied to a case, they produce a "range." A range might be 51-63 months, for example. The sentencing range is determined by matching two numbers on a chart known as the "Sentencing Table."[13] One of the numbers is the offense level. The other is the criminal history category. The "offense level" is supposed to reflect the seriousness of the offense. The criminal history category reflects the number and seriousness of the defendant's prior convictions. A sentencing court is *required* to consider this range before imposing sentence. It is therefore important that the court correctly calculate the sentencing range suggested by the guidelines.

How the offense of conviction affects the guideline range

The guidelines measure the seriousness of an offense in two different ways. First, they look to the offense of conviction to determine the offense guideline. This can be critical. For example, a public official who took a bribe might be convicted of accepting a bribe in violation of 18 U.S.C. § 201(b), or of accepting a gratuity, in violation of 18 U.S.C. § 201(c). Pleading to a gratuity count will result in a lower guideline range, because the offense guideline for a gratuity conviction has a base offense level of 9 (11, if the defendant is a public official),[14] whereas the offense guideline for a bribery conviction has a base offense level of 12 (14, if the defendant is a public official).[15] The higher the total offense level, the higher the sentencing range.

"Relevant conduct"

Selection of the offense guideline is controlled by the offense of conviction. Almost all other guideline decisions are determined by "relevant conduct." "Relevant conduct" looks beyond the offense of conviction to what actually happened. For some cases, "relevant conduct" means what the defendant did to commit the offense, or to prepare to commit the offense, or to try to avoid being caught after committing the offense.[16] In many (if not most) cases, "relevant conduct" includes much more.

The fraud, theft, tax, and drug guidelines use amounts of money or quantities of drugs to measure the seriousness of the offense. In cases like these, "relevant conduct" can include conduct which is not part of the offense of conviction. The guidelines look beyond the offense of conviction to other acts or omissions which were part of the same "course of conduct" or "common scheme or plan."[17]

For example, a defendant convicted on a $1,000 fraud count could end up with a higher guideline range than another defendant convicted on a $100,000 fraud count. If the $1,000 fraud count was part of a "scheme" that included 200 such frauds, the "relevant conduct" would be $200,000. If the $100,000 fraud was not part of a larger scheme, then its "relevant conduct" would be only $100,000. Because the "relevant conduct" for the $1,000 fraud would then be higher than the "relevant conduct" for the $100,000 fraud, it will most likely produce a higher guideline range.

"Relevant conduct" sometimes includes things done by other people. This kind of relevant conduct applies when a defendant worked with other people to commit an offense. The guidelines call it "jointly undertaken criminal activity." A defendant does not have to be charged with a conspiracy for this type of relevant conduct to apply. A defendant does not even have to know the other people. Nor does he have to know everything about what they did. Before a defendant can receive a higher guideline level for things other people did, several factors must be present. First, several people must have worked together to commit the offense. Second, the things that someone else did must have been "reasonably foreseeable" to the defendant. In other words, if the defendant had stopped to think about it, would he have been surprised at what the others did? Finally, the things that other people did must have been "in furtherance of the jointly undertaken criminal activity."[18] That means that they must have been done to help accomplish the same overall illegal plan the defendant helped carry out.

For example, if a defendant unloaded one crate from a truck full of marijuana, all the marijuana from the truck could be "relevant conduct."

The entire truckload could be "relevant conduct" if three conditions are met. First, other people had to be involved with the offense. Second, it must have been "reasonably foreseeable" to the defendant that the entire truck was filled with marijuana. Finally, unloading the one crate must have been part of an effort to distribute the whole truckload.

"Relevant conduct" does not have to be described in the indictment. It can involve conduct described only in counts dismissed under a plea agreement. *It can even include conduct for which a defendant has been acquitted.* The only limit on how high "relevant conduct" can push an offense level is the maximum sentence allowed by the statute of conviction. No guideline offense level can exceed the limit placed by statute on the counts of conviction.

The guidelines "sentencing range"

The guidelines calculate a suggested sentencing range that applies to an entire case. They do not determine suggested ranges for particular counts. Once a court determines a range, the judge must "consider" it, along with the other factors listed in 18 U.S.C. § 3553(a), before imposing sentence.

The guidelines tell the judge how to calculate a sentencing range for the entire case. After the court "considers" that range, along with the other § 3553(a) factors, it must formally impose sentence separately on each count. If the guideline range is less than the statutory maximum of each count, the guidelines recommend that the court impose the sentences to run concurrently with each other. When sentences are imposed concurrently the defendant serves them all at the same time.

The guidelines recommend that a court impose sentences to run consecutively if that is necessary to achieve a sentence within the guideline range. When sentences are imposed consecutively, they are served one after the other. For example, the statutory maximum for one count of conspiring to commit an offense against the United States (18 U.S.C. § 371) is five years. If a defendant were convicted on two such counts, the court could impose a guideline sentence of 84 months (seven years) only by running the sentences consecutively. However if the guideline range was 11 to 15 years, the court could not impose a sentence higher than ten years in all. A court may not exceed the statutory maximum for any count. The total sentence for the case must stay within the total maximum for all the counts.

Choosing the correct guideline manual

The Sentencing Commission has issued changes to the Guidelines Manual almost every year since the first edition came out in 1987. The changes are compiled into a new version of the Manual on November 1 of every year. The law requires courts to use the version of the sentencing manual in effect on the day a defendant is sentenced.[19] Sometimes, however, the manual in effect on the day of sentencing produces a guideline range that is higher than it would be if the court had used the manual in effect on the day the offense was committed. When this happens, the court must use the manual in effect on the day the defendant committed the offense.[20] This is required by the Constitution's *Ex Post Facto* Clause.

To check whether there is an *Ex Post Facto* problem, the court may have to make two calculations. The court will calculate the range using the manual in effect on the day of sentencing. It will then calculate the range using the manual in effect on the day the defendant committed the offense. The court then compares the two ranges and uses the lower one. A court will not pick one guideline section from one manual and another from the other manual, to come up with the lowest sentence possible. This is called the "one book" rule.

There is one important exception to the "one book" rule. A court will apply a "clarifying amendment" from a later manual even if it uses an earlier manual. A "clarifying amendment" is a change which explains what an earlier guideline meant. A court will apply a clarifying amendment to an earlier manual, because the amendment does not really change the earlier guideline. It just explains what the guideline meant all along.

Applying the guidelines

Step One: Select the offense guideline

The first step is to select the offense guideline for each offense of conviction.[21] The offense guidelines are found in Chapter Two of the Guidelines Manual. The Statutory Index lists the offense guidelines applicable to most federal offenses. It can be found in Appendix A to the Manual. If an offense is not listed in the Statutory Index, then the guidelines provide that the "most analogous" offense guideline should be used.[22] If the defendant has a plea agreement that stipulates to an offense that is more serious than the offense of conviction, the guidelines require the court to use the offense guideline for that more serious offense.

Step Two: Determine the base offense level

After selecting the offense guideline, the next step is to determine the "base offense level." The "base offense level" is the minimum offense level for a particular offense. It usually does not depend on any of the details of the case. For example, the base offense level for insider trading is Level 8.[23] If a defendant is convicted of insider trading, he will start out with eight offense levels, no matter what happened in the case.

Some offense guidelines set the base offense level based upon an amount of money or drugs. For example, USSG § 2D1.1(c) uses drug weight to set the base offense level. In tax cases, the base offense level is at least level 6, but could be higher, depending on the amount of taxes involved. Only drugs or money which qualify as "relevant conduct" are used to set the base offense level.

Sometimes, the base offense level is established by the offense level for an underlying offense. This is true for money laundering cases, for example.[24] If the money laundered is from a fraud, then the fraud guideline sets the offense level for money laundering. Occasionally, a guideline will set a minimum base offense level, but will provide that the offense level of an underlying offense will apply if it is higher. This is true for RICO cases.[25]

Step Three: Specific offense characteristics

The next step is to see if any "specific offense characteristic" (SOC) applies. SOCs add (or sometimes subtract) offense levels to the base offense level. The Sentencing Commission lists different SOCs for each offense guideline. For example, in fraud cases, the victim loss is an SOC. This SOC ranges from no increase in offense level where there is no loss, to a 30-level increase when the loss exceeds $100 million.[26]

It is important to remember that an SOC applies only to the offense guideline in which it is found. For example, a drug offense SOC provides for a two-level increase if a gun "was possessed."[27] Therefore, a defendant in a drug case will receive a two-level increase if a firearm "was possessed." (The defendant does not have to be the person who "possessed" the firearm. He will receive two levels if the firearm "was possessed" by anyone for whose conduct he is responsible.) However, because the "Promoting a Commercial Sex Act" guideline, § 2G1.1, has no similar SOC, a defendant in that kind of a case where a gun "was possessed" does not receive an increase in offense level.

Step Four: Cross references and special instructions

Occasionally, the offense guideline contains a "cross reference" or "special instruction." "Cross references" tell the court to apply a different offense guideline under certain circumstances. For example, USSG § 2D1.7 normally applies to sales of drug paraphernalia. Although the base offense level for this offense is normally 12, a "cross reference" requires the court to use the drug offense guideline in some paraphernalia cases, if that results in a higher offense level.[28]

"Special instructions" tell the court how to apply the guidelines in particular situations. Some special instructions relate to the calculation of fines. The price rigging offense guideline has an instruction like that.[29] So does the guideline for use of a firearm during and in relation to certain crimes.[30] Other offense guidelines instruct the court to calculate the guideline offense level as if the defendant were convicted on a separate count for each victim, even though he was not. The guideline for the unlawful production of weapons of mass destruction has that kind of instruction.[31]

Step Five: Adjustments related to the nature of the victim, the defendant's role in the offense, and obstruction of justice

Next, the Court applies adjustments that have to do with the victim, the defendant's role in the offense, and obstruction of justice.[32] These adjustments are found in Chapter Three, Parts A, B, and C of the Sentencing Guidelines Manual. Unlike the offense guidelines in Chapter Two of the Manual, these adjustments apply to all offenses. For example, USSG § 3B1.1 adds between two and four levels based on a defendant's leadership role. This adjustment can be added no matter which offense guideline applies.

There are also adjustments which apply based on the nature of the victim. A defendant can receive additional levels if the victim was especially "vulnerable," for example.[33] Levels are also added if the victim was a government official.[34] An adjustment applies if the victim was "restrained,"[35] or if the offense involved or promoted terrorism.[36]

Role in the offense adjustments can either increase or decrease the offense level. If the defendant was an organizer, leader, manager, or supervisor of at least one other participant, the court must increase his offense level from between two and four levels. The amount of increase depends on the nature of the defendant's role and the number of people involved in the offense, or how extensive the offense was.[37] A defendant's offense level is decreased between two and four levels if his role in the offense was comparatively "minimal," "minor," or somewhere in between.[38] In drug cases, defendants who receive minor or minimal role adjustments also qualify for additional decreases.[39]

The guidelines also call for a role-in-the-offense increase if the defendant abused a position of trust or used a special skill.[40] There is also an upward adjustment if the defendant used someone under the age of 18 to help commit the offense, or to avoid detection or apprehension.[41]

Before the abuse of a position of trust adjustment applies, the government must prove two things. First, the defendant must have held a "position of trust." A "position of trust" is not the same as "being trusted." This adjustment does not apply simply because a victim trusted a defendant. The defendant must hold a *position* of trust. For example, a corporate officer holds a position of trust with respect to his corporation. Second, being in a position of trust must have helped the defendant commit the offense. For example, being a corporate officer might help a defendant steal funds to which he had access because he was an officer.

The use of a special skill adjustment applies to defendants who have "special skills," such as lawyers, chemists, doctors, pilots, and accountants. But having a special skill is not enough to qualify for this adjustment. The special skill must help the defendant commit the offense. A chemist convicted of tax evasion would not receive this adjustment. You don't need to be a chemist to evade taxes. A chemist convicted of manufacturing controlled substances, on the other hand, might receive it. The question would be whether his special knowledge of chemistry helped him commit the offense.

The obstruction of justice adjustment is found at USSG § 3C1.1. It is most often applied against defendants who testify falsely in their own defense. Not all defendants who testify receive this adjustment. The Court must first find that they committed perjury. It is a risk that all defendants must consider before taking the stand. The adjustment is also applied to other obstructive behavior, such as destroying evidence, or pressuring or threatening witnesses.

Step Six: Grouping

Whenever there is more than one count of conviction, the offense levels for each count or group of counts must be "combined." The offense levels must be combined for the guidelines to determine an offense level that applies to the entire case. There are two ways that the guidelines combine offense levels from different counts to determine the offense level for the case. The first way is by "grouping." The second way is by taking the offense level for the most serious count, and then adding levels to it. The number of levels added to the offense level for the most serious count depends on the seriousness of the other counts.[42]

Counts can be "grouped" if they are "closely related."[43] Several kinds of counts can be grouped. Counts are grouped when their offense levels are largely determined by a quantity of something.[44] For example, if a defendant pleads guilty to two counts of possession of marijuana with intent to distribute, those counts are considered together. The total amount of marijuana from both counts is added up and used to establish the base offense level for the "group." Counts of fraud or tax evasion would group this way.

Counts can also be grouped when their offense levels are not largely determined by quantity. Courts look to a number of factors to make grouping decisions in these kinds of cases. First, a court would look at whether the crimes had the same victim or victims. If they did, the court would look to whether the offenses involved the same acts or transactions. It would also look to whether they were part of a common scheme or plan. If both of these factors were present, the counts would group.[45] Consider a case in which a defendant trespassed on government property and stole something from the government. The defendant was convicted on one count of trespassing on government property and another count of theft of government property. The counts would group because both factors are present. First, the victim of each count is the same – the government. Second, both counts are part of the same scheme – a scheme to steal something from the government. When counts are grouped in this way, the offense level for the group is the offense level for the most serious count.[46]

Counts are also grouped when one count is conduct that is used to determine the offense level for another count.[47] For example, the base offense level for a money laundering count is the offense level for the underlying offense. If the underlying offense is a drug offense, then the money laundering and drug offenses would be grouped. When counts are grouped in this way, the offense level for the group is the offense level for the most serious count.

Some offenses are never grouped together. Some of these crimes are identified in USSG §3D1.2. For example, burglary counts are not grouped, even though their offense level depends on the loss to the victim. USSG § 2B2.1 is the burglary guideline. Generally, violent crimes or offenses against persons are not grouped. Assaults, robberies, and sexual offenses are not grouped. Some non-violent offenses also do not group. These include fraudulently acquiring naturalization, citizenship or residency documents, payment to obtain public office, or escape from custody or confinement.[48]

If counts are not grouped, the court will use USSG § 3D1.4 to determine a combined offense level. For example, if a defendant was convicted of conspiracy to commit murder, several drug distribution counts, and a bank robbery, not all the counts would group. The drug distribution counts would group with each other. But they would not group with the other counts. The murder and bank robbery counts would not group with any count. The court would therefore calculate an offense level for the drug distribution group. It would also separately calculate an offense level for the murder group and one for the robbery group. The court would then combine these offense levels. Even though there was only one count of robbery and one count of murder, the guidelines think of them as separate "groups" when it combines them.

When a court combines offense levels, it first looks to the offense level for the most serious group. It then compares that offense level to the offense level for each of the other groups. When the offense level for a group is between one and eight levels less serious than the most serious group, the combined offense level will be raised.[49] When a group is nine or more levels less serious than the most serious offense, it does not cause the combined offense level to increase.[50]

When a defendant is convicted of more than one crime, and those counts cannot be grouped, the combined offense level is determined solely by the counts of conviction. For example, if a defendant is convicted of four bank robberies, his combined offense level will be based on the four counts of conviction. This is so, even if the government has evidence that the defendant committed nine bank robberies. The court, however, might consider the other bank robberies in deciding whether to impose a sentence that is higher than the top of the guideline range.

Step Seven: Acceptance of responsibility

The last step in calculating the offense level is to determine whether the "acceptance of responsibility" adjustment applies.[51] Defendants who accept responsibility are entitled to at least a two-level reduction in offense level.[52] Sometimes, defendants are entitled to a three-level reduction.[53]

The two-level reduction is most often given to defendants who plead guilty. But pleading guilty is no guarantee. Defendants who plead guilty are sometimes denied credit for acceptance of responsibility. Defendants who try to withdraw their pleas prior to sentencing have been denied the credit. So have defendants who have made statements denying guilt after they pleaded guilty. Defendants who obstruct justice or commit other crimes after pleading guilty are often denied the credit, too.

Sometimes, but not very often, a court will give credit for accepting responsibility to a defendant who went to trial. Defendants who receive this credit after going to trial usually have not disagreed with the prosecutor's version of what happened. Instead, they are people who made only a legal argument at trial that what they did was not a crime.

A defendant is entitled to an additional level reduction for acceptance of responsibility, for a total of three, if he meets three conditions. First, he must have an offense level of 16 or higher. The level is measured right before the credit is applied. Second, he must timely notify the prosecution of his intent to plead guilty, "thereby permitting the government to avoid preparing for trial and permitting the government and the court to allocate their resources efficiently."[54] Finally, a court may grant this third level downward adjustment only if the prosecutor files a motion which states that defendant meets the criteria for the additional level.

Step Eight: Criminal history category

A defendant's guideline range is determined by two factors. The first factor is the offense level. The second factor is the criminal history category. We have already discussed how the court determines a defendant's offense level. In this section, we discuss how the court determines the criminal history category. A higher criminal history category means a higher guideline range.

A court calculates a defendant's criminal history category using criminal history points. Defendants receive "points" for prior sentences. The number of points a defendant receives partially depends on the length of each prior sentence. A defendant receives three points for each prior sentence of at least 13 months.[55] A defendant receives two points for each prior sentence of at least sixty days.[56] Otherwise a defendant receives one point for a prior sentence.[57] A defendant receives two more points if he committed his current offense while he was on probation, parole, supervised release, imprisonment, work release or escape status.[58] The court adds another two points if the defendant committed the current offense when he was in prison. The court also adds up to two more points if the defendant committed the current offense less than two years after he completed a sentence of at least 60 days.[59]

Some sentences are too old to be counted. A sentence of more than 13 months does not count if the sentence was imposed more than 15 years before the defendant began to commit the current offense. There is one exception to this rule. A sentence imposed more than 15 years ago counts if the defendant committed the current offense less then 15 years after he was released from prison on the prior sentence. A similar ten-year rule applies to prior sentences of 13 months or less.

A prior sentence of probation normally counts for one criminal history point. For example, if a defendant was sentenced to three years' probation, he would normally receive one point. However, if the court later revoked probation and sentenced the defendant to 14 months in prison, he would receive three points.

Some minor offenses never add points. Sentences for hitchhiking, loitering and public intoxication never count. Other sentences only count if the defendant received at least 30 days' imprisonment or one year of probation, *or* if the prior offense was similar to the current offense. Sentences for careless or reckless driving, disorderly conduct, contempt of court, gambling, prostitution and trespassing are treated like this.

A prior sentence that punished conduct that is part of the current offense does not count. In other words, if conduct underlying the prior sentence is "relevant conduct" for the current offense, no points are added. For example, when a defendant is prosecuted in both state and federal court for the same acts, the defendant receives no points for the prior state sentence.

Cases that ended in diversion or deferred prosecution usually don't add points. The exception is cases in which the defendant entered a formal plea of guilty or nolo contendere.

Sentences imposed in foreign countries do not count. Neither do sentences for expunged, reversed, or invalid convictions. Sentences which are "set aside" for errors of law, or because the defendants are innocent, do not count. Prior sentences usually do not count if the defendant committed the offense when he was under 18. However, when juveniles receive adult sentences of 13 months or more, they do count as priors. Sentences imposed on juveniles also count if the defendants began their current offenses within five years of completing the juvenile sentences.

There are six criminal history categories. Category I is for defendants with either zero or one criminal history point. Category VI is for defendants with more than 13 points. Criminal history points affect a defendant's guideline range. A defendant in Category I will have a lower guideline range than will a defendant with the same offense level who is in a higher criminal history category.

Sometimes, a defendant's criminal history score exaggerates or understates the seriousness of his criminal record. A defendant may have a lot of points because of many minor brushes with the law. The high criminal history category may make his priors seem more serious than they really are. In that case, a guideline policy statement[60] suggests that a "downward departure" may a appropriate.[61] Another defendant may have a long criminal history, but few prior sentences that count. This can happen when a defendant has many foreign or juvenile convictions that do not count. In such a case, a guideline policy statement suggests that an "upward departure" may be appropriate.

Step Nine: The guideline range

Once the court has arrived at the applicable offense level and criminal history category, it is a simple matter to determine the guideline range. The court just turns to the Sentencing Table at the beginning of Chapter Five of the Guidelines Manual and goes to the intersection of the appropriate offense level line with the criminal history category column. The Table is also in the Appendix of this booklet. The range is given in months of imprisonment. For example, if the offense level is 24 and the criminal history category is III, the range is 63-78 months. A 0-6 month range means that the sentencing guidelines recommend a sentence somewhere between probation and six months' imprisonment.

There are two exceptions to this method of arriving at the guideline range. The first is where the guideline range would come out higher than the statutory maximum. For example, if a defendant is convicted on one count of money laundering, a 20-year statutory maximum applies. If the defendant's offense level was 34 and his criminal history category was VI, the range would normally be 262-327 months. However, because the statutory maximum is 20 years (240 months), the 262-327-month range does not apply. Instead, 240 months becomes the recommended guideline sentence.[62]

If the same defendant is being sentenced on one money laundering count and one drug count, the court would be able to impose a sentence within the guideline range if it wanted to. The court could construct a sentence within this range by running part of the sentences consecutively. For example, if the drug count had a statutory maximum of 20 years, then the court could impose a 20-year sentence on each count. The Court could run part of one sentence consecutively to achieve a sentence within the 262-327-month guideline range.[63]

The second exception is where the range is lower than a mandatory minimum sentence. For example, if the offense level is 22 and the criminal history category is I, the guideline range would normally be 41-51 months. However, if the defendant was subject to a five-year mandatory minimum sentence, the recommended guideline sentence becomes 60 months (five years).[64] Mandatory life sentences also trump any lower sentence suggested by the guidelines. Mandatory life is required by certain murder and drug statutes and under the "three strikes" law.[65] There is no parole for defendants sentenced for crimes committed on or after November 1, 1987, which is when the Sentencing Reform Act, the law that established the Guidelines, went into effect. A person receiving a life sentence will die in prison unless the sentence is later changed for some reason.

Special situations – career offenders, ACCA, repeat and dangerous sex offenders, Three Strikes, and Mandatory Minimums

The guidelines generally determine the sentencing range by calculating the offense level and the criminal history category in the ways we have already discussed. This method usually produces a sentence that any reasonable person would consider punitive enough. Sometimes, though, Congress wants to make sure that the guideline range is even harsher. Congress has mandated extremely high guideline ranges for four types of defendants. The Sentencing Commission has adjusted the guidelines to comply. The first type of defendant is the "career offender." To be a "career offender," a defendant must meet three conditions. He must have been at least 18 years old when he committed his current offense. His current offense must be a crime of violence or a "controlled sub-stance" offense. Finally, he must have two prior convictions for crimes of violence or controlled substance offenses. The Career Offender guideline sets offense levels based on statutory maximums.[66] It also places all "career offenders" in Criminal History Category VI.

"Armed career criminals" must receive sentences of at least 15 years' imprisonment. They may be sentenced up to life in prison. An "armed career criminal" is someone who violates 18 U.S.C. § 922(g) and meets other conditions set by § 924(e) (the Armed Career Criminal Act, also known as "ACCA"). Section 922(g) mainly applies to gun possession by previously-convicted felons. Explaining these offenses is beyond the scope of this booklet. The guideline offense level for ACCA defendants is determined by USSG §4B1.4. This guideline requires the court to calculate a defendant's offense level using the one of several methods that produces the greatest offense level. The first method is to deter-mine the defendant's normal guideline level. The second uses the "career offender" guideline, if that is applicable. The third imposes an offense level of 33 or 34. The ACCA guideline also controls a defendant's criminal history category. It requires a criminal history category of at least IV. In some cases it requires a court to use Category VI.

Repeat sexual offenders are subject to statutory maximums which are twice as long as first offenders.[67] The guidelines take this into account through USSG § 4B1.5. This is the guideline for "repeat and dangerous sex offenders against minors." This guideline sets the offense level based on the statutory maximum. It requires at a criminal history category of at least Category V.

Some laws require courts to impose a sentence that is no less than a certain number of years. Such sentences are called "mandatory minimums." Mandatory minimum sentences are the most common way that Congress makes sure that some defendants receive harsher sentences than their guidelines would otherwise require. For example, a defendant convicted of growing 100 or more marijuana plants must be sentenced to at least five years in prison, no matter how much the plants weigh.[68] If a defendant grew 100 marijuana plants that each produced 100 grams of useable marijuana, he would have grown 10 kilograms of marijuana. This normally results in a base offense level 16. If this defendant received no other levels and was in Criminal History Category I, his guideline range would normally be 21-27 months. However, because of the mandatory minimum, the court would have to impose a five-year (60 month) sentence on that count.

Other § 3553(a) Factors

After the sentencing court calculates the guideline range, it must "consider" that range, along with the other factors listed in 18 U.S.C. § 3553(a).[69] Those factors are the "nature and circumstances of the offense and the history and characteristics of the defendant,"[70] the purposes of sentencing,[71] "the kinds of sentences available,"[72] the policy statements issued by the Sentencing Commission, such as those related to departures,[73] "the need to avoid unwarranted sentence disparities among defendants with similar records who have been found guilty of similar conduct,"[74] and "the need to provide restitution to any victims of the offense."[75]

Suffice it to say that at this point judges have much more discretion to impose a sentence outside the guideline range than they did before

Booker. We discuss the nature of that discretion at length in the section of this chapter called "Appeals from Sentencing Decisions."

Departures and Variances

One of the seven factors a sentencing court must "consider" is the Sentencing Commission's policy statements. The sections of the Sentencing Guidelines Manual that deal with "departures" are all "policy statements." When the guidelines were mandatory, a "departure" was the only way a court could impose a sentence outside the guideline range. "Departures" were the way that the guidelines dealt with situations that were either not covered by the guidelines at all, or which were not adequately covered by them. When a defendant qualifies for a "departure," the guidelines themselves recognize that it may be appropriate for a court to impose a sentence that is lower or higher than the otherwise recommended range. When a court lowers the offense level or criminal history category for this reason, it is called a "downward departure." When it raises one of them for this reason, it is called an "upward departure." When a court "departs," it does not have to say that it is departing up or down any particular number of offense levels or criminal history categories. It can simply depart to a sentence that is higher or lower than the guideline range. When the guidelines were still mandatory, "departures" were the only way a court could impose a sentence outside the guideline range.

Now that the guidelines are advisory, it is less important whether a particular mitigating or aggravating factor would justify a "departure." That is because courts may now sentence below or above the guideline range if they think that is necessary to achieve a sentence that is "sufficient, but not greater than necessary" to achieve the goals of sentencing – regardless of whether there are grounds for a "departure" under the guidelines. A sentence above or below the guideline range that is not supported by a "departure" is called a "variance."

Although a court may now impose a below-guideline sentence even when guideline policy statements provide no basis to 'depart,' policy statements are still important. Just as courts are still required to "consider" the recommended guideline sentencing range, they are also required to "consider" guideline "policy statements." "Policy statements" include the Sentencing Commission's guidance on departures. If a mitigating factor would have justified a downward departure under the mandatory guideline system, it may be easier to justify a lower sentence to a court.

There are several factors which sentencing guideline policy statements provide may never support departures. They include: race, sex, religion, lack of youthful guidance, drug or alcohol dependence, and post-sentencing rehabilitation. Courts must "consider" this recommendation. But now that the guidelines are no longer mandatory, courts may, in appropriate cases, rely on these formerly excluded factors to impose a sentence that is outside the guideline range.

There are three situations in which guideline policy statements state that departures may be appropriate. The first is where the case involves a factor that is not mentioned by the guidelines at all. Such factors are likely to be unique to the case in question. The second situation is where a case involves a factor for which a policy statement "encourages" departures. Encouraged downward departures are listed in USSG §§ 5K2.1 – 5K2.18 and § 5K2.20. Some of the circumstances for which the guidelines encourage downward departures are:

- The victim's wrongful conduct provoked the offense.

- The defendant committed the offense to avoid a greater harm. The guidelines give "mercy killing" as an example of this.

- The defendant was forced to commit the offense. This departure is helpful when there was coercion, but not enough to warrant an acquittal.

- The offense was out of character for the defendant. The guidelines call this "aberrant behavior."

- The defendant's diminished mental capacity contributed to the offense. "Diminished mental capacity" refers to psychological problems. It also covers very low intelligence. The guidelines recognize two kinds of diminished capacity. One kind of diminished capacity makes it difficult for a defendant to control his behavior. The other kind makes it difficult for a defendant to understand that what he did was wrong or to "exercise the power of reason." This departure is encouraged only for non-violent offenses and for "diminished capacity" which was not caused by voluntary drug or other intoxicant use. It is also not generally available to sex offenses.

- The defendant voluntarily disclosed the offense.

The guidelines encourage *upward* departures for things such as extreme conduct, abduction or unlawful restraint, extreme psychological injury, and significantly endangering the public welfare. Some of the guidelines in Chapter Two also mention "encouraged departures" for specific types of offenses. Most of these point upward, but some encourage downward departures.

The third situation in which guideline policy statements recognize that departures may be appropriate is where a case involves a "discouraged factor" to an extraordinary degree. The guidelines say that these factors are "not ordinarily relevant" to whether a court should depart. Departures based on such factors are recommended only if they are present to an extraordinary extent. Factors for which departures are "discouraged" include:

- A defendant's age;

- A defendant's education;

- A defendant's skills;

- A defendant's current physical, mental or emotional condition;

- A defendant's civic and charitable contributions;

- A defendant's employment record;

- A defendant's family ties and responsibilities.

These factors are "discouraged" as reasons for departure because they are more common. For example, it is not unusual for a defendant facing sentencing to have emotional problems. Children and spouses often suffer when one of their family is sent to prison. Policy statements recommend that courts not depart for these reasons unless the emotional problem or the suffering of the spouse or children is extraordinary.

Sometimes policy statements recommend that courts consider departures based on a factor that the guidelines have considered. This can happen when the factor is present to a degree that the guidelines did not consider. For example, the guidelines provide for a downward adjustment for acceptance of responsibility. Some courts have departed downward for extraordinary acceptance of responsibility. When a court "departs" for this reason, it means that it lowers the offense level even more than the two or three levels provided by the guidelines. Courts have found extraordinary acceptance of responsibility is several situations. Defendants who have begun to pay restitution before they knew they were under investigation for an offense have gotten this departure. So have defendants who have taken steps to rehabilitate themselves before being sentenced. Now that the guidelines are no longer mandatory, courts may chose to impose sentences below the recommended range for reasons that the Sentencing Commission took into account, so long as they "consider" the guidelines, policy statements, and other factors required by 18 U.S.C. § 3553(a), and so long as they explain why the lower sentence is "sufficient, but not greater than necessary" to achieve the goals of sentencing.

A defendant also may receive a downward "departure" if he helps the government prosecute or investigate someone else. A guideline policy statement recommends that a court not depart for this reason unless the prosecution files a motion that states that the defendant provided "substantial assistance." Normally, a defendant can not force the government to file a "substantial assistance" motion. There are two, and in some Circuits, three exceptions to this rule. The first is when the government refuses to file a motion for a unconstitutional reason, such as a defendant's race. The second is when the government has agreed in a plea agreement to file the motion, and then does not. It is unusual for the government to promise in advance to file a "substantial assistance motion." Plea agreements often mention conditions under which the government will file "substantial assistance" motions – but usually give the government sole discretion to determine whether those conditions have been met.

In some Circuits, there is a third exception to the general rule. This exception can help defendants with cooperation agreements which provide that the government will file the motion if it believes the defendant's cooperation amounts to "substantial assistance." Agreements like these are hard to enforce. The government can always say that it did not believe that the defendant's cooperation was "substantial assistance." In some Circuits a defendant can force the prosecution to file a departure motion if he can demonstrate that the prosecution's refusal to file the motion was made in "bad faith." The defendant must prove that his cooperation met the prosecution's standards for "substantial assistance," but the prosecution refused to file the motion anyway.

Unless one of these conditions apply, a defendant cannot force the government to file a departure motion. This is not to suggest that substantial assistance motions are rare. They are not. The latest figures available (the ones for 2006), reflect that a government substantial assistance motion is the most common reason for departure. Courts departed in 14.4% of the sentences imposed that year, in response to "substantial assistance" motions.

Now that the guidelines are no longer mandatory, courts have the authority to impose lower sentences to reward cooperation – even where the prosecution has refused to file a departure motion. The one exception to this rule is where a mandatory minimum sentence applies. In that situation, a government motion is *required* before a court can impose sentence below that minimum.

"Substantial assistance" motions, cooperation agreements, and the safety valve

There are two exceptions to laws which require mandatory minimum sentences. One applies when the prosecutor makes a "substantial assistance" motion. This exception applies to all mandatory minimum cases. The other applies only to drug cases. It is known as the "safety valve."

"Substantial assistance" motions

"Substantial assistance" motions reward defendants who "cooperate" with the government. "Cooperate" means to help the federal government investigate or prosecute other people. There are two kinds of "substantial assistance" motions. One kind permits courts to go below mandatory minimums. That kind of motion is authorized by 18 U.S.C. § 3553(e). The other kind asks courts to depart below the guideline range – but not below a mandatory minimum. That kind of motion is authorized by USSG § 5K1.1.

Prosecutors do not file departure motions for all cooperators. A prosecutor will file a motion only if the cooperation was "substantial." What is "substantial" in one prosecutor's office may not be "substantial" in another office. All prosecutors think that testifying against another person is "substantial." Some prosecutors think that talking about another person is not "substantial" if it does not lead to an arrest or conviction.

In a case involving a mandatory minimum sentence, a substantial assistance departure motion can give a court the power to impose a sentence as low as probation in some but not all cases. A court can impose a lower sentence without a substantial assistance motion in a case that does not involve a mandatory minimum sentence. But it is more likely that a court will impose a lower sentence if the government files a motion. A court will usually impose a lower sentence when the government files a departure motion. But not always. Departure motions do not *require* courts to impose lower sentences. Sometimes prosecutors make recommendations in their motions. A court also does not have to go along with a prosecutor's recommendation. It is up to the court how low to go. In some cases defense counsel can pursuade the court to go even lower than recommended by the prosecutor.

Cooperation agreements

Plea agreements sometimes require defendants to cooperate with the government. These are called "cooperation agreements." Cooperation agreements provide different kinds of benefits to defendants. Sometimes the prosecution promises to file a substantial assistance departure motion. If the government makes the promise without any conditions, it *must* file the motion. More often, a promise by the prosecution comes with conditions attached. The usual condition is that the defendant's cooperation must be "substantial." Usually it is entirely up to the prosecutor to decide what counts as being "substantial." Sometimes the government promises only to "consider" filing a motion. These kinds of agreements often lead to departure motions, but they are not guarantees.

The "safety valve"

There are no mandatory minimums in drug cases for defendants who quality for the "safety valve." If a defendant qualifies for the safety valve, the court may sentence him below the mandatory minimum.[76]

Most defendants who qualify for the safety valve also qualify for a two-level decrease in their offense levels.[77] There is one exception to this rule. A safety valve decrease cannot take a defendant's offense level below Level 17.[78]

A safety valve reduction is not the same thing as a departure. A defendant who qualifies for the safety valve will usually receive a lower sentence, because his guideline range will usually be lower. It will usually be lower, because no mandatory minimum will make it higher, and because he will receive a two-level decrease.

The prosecution does not have to file any motion to qualify a defendant for the "safety valve." A defendant must meet five conditions:

1. Not more than one criminal history point;

2. Defendant did not use or threaten violence; defendant did not possess a dangerous weapon in connection with the offense;

3. No one was killed or seriously injured by the offense;

4. Defendant not an organizer, leader, manager or supervisor of other people involved in the offense; and

5. Prior to sentencing, defendant tells the prosecution everything he knows about his offense and "relevant conduct."

The requirement that a defendant talk to the prosecution about his own offense and "relevant conduct" does not mean that he must give the government new information. It does mean, however, that sometimes a defendant must tell the prosecution about the criminal conduct of other people. A defendant does not have to testify against any one to qualify for the safety valve.

Probation, split sentences, and community or home confinement

Now that the guidelines are advisory, the restrictions they used to impose on probation, split sentences, and community or home confinement, no longer limit courts in the same way. Courts now have the authority to impose these kinds of sentences in almost any case – even if there is no reason to "depart." The exception is where a statute prohibits a certain kind of sentence. Because a court must still "consider" the guidelines, it is important to understand how these restrictions work.

The guidelines recommend probation only if the range is in "Zone A" or "Zone B" of the Sentencing Table. "Zone A" means the guideline range is between zero and six months. A sentence of probation would be within the guideline range, because a sentence of zero months is a sentence within the range. A sentence within this range also does not have to have home or community confinement as a term of probation.[79] "Community confinement" means a halfway house.

Defendants in "Zone B" also may receive sentences of probation that are within the guideline range. "Zone B" ranges have low ends between one and six months, and high ends of 12 months or less. For defendants in "Zone B," for a probation sentence to be within the guideline range, it must include some kind of confinement as a term of probation. That confinement can be in a halfway house or home confinement. "Zone B" sentences may allow work release from the confinement without being outside the guideline range.[80]

Defendants in "Zone C" may receive what is sometimes called a "split sentence," and still be within the guideline range. "Zone C" ranges have low ends greater than six months, but less than 12 months. Defendants in Zone C may receive sentences within the guideline range which require them to serve at least half of the minimum term in prison, and the other half in community confinement or home detention, as a condition of supervised release.[81] For example, if a defendant has a guideline range of 8-14 months, putting him in "Zone C," the judge could give a sentence within the guideline range that includes four months' imprisonment and supervised release that included a condition that the defendant serve four months in a half-way house or in home detention.

The guidelines recommend that defendants in Zone D not be sentenced to terms of probation. Zone D ranges have low ends of at least 12 months. After *Booker*, some creative lawyers have successfully urged judges to impose probation or split sentences for people whose guidelines fall within Zone D. For example, judges have imposed sentences of a year and a day of incarceration followed by supervised release, with a year's home confinement as a condition of supervised release, rather than two-year advisory guideline prison sentences.[82]

When the defendant is already serving a sentence

Some defendants are already serving sentences for other crimes when they are sentenced. Sometimes the guidelines recommend a sentence that runs consecutively to the first sentence. If the court accepts that recommendation, the new sentence will not even start until the defendant completes the first sentence. In other cases, the guidelines recommend concurrent sentences. That means that if the court accepts the recommendation, the defendant will serve both sentences at the same time, at least starting from when the second sentence is imposed.[83] In other cases, the guidelines make no specific recommendation, other than that courts use their discretion to impose concurrent or consecutive sentences, or sentences that are a little of both.

The guidelines recommend consecutive sentences for crimes committed while the person was already in prison, or on work release, furlough, or escape status.[84] The guidelines recommend concurrent sentences if two conditions are met. First, the defendant must not have committed the offense in prison, or on work release, furlough, or escape status. Second, the guidelines for the current offense must take the earlier offense conduct into account. This can happen when a defendant is prosecuted for a federal offense after he was prosecuted for a state offense which punishes some or all of the same conduct.

Sometimes a defendant is serving a sentence for an unrelated crime that he did not commit in prison, etc. For these cases, the guidelines make no recommendation, other than that courts use their discretion to run the sentence consecutively or concurrently, or a combination of the two. The guidelines recommend that judges decide what result is most fair in such cases.

Supervised release

There is no parole for defendants sentenced for crimes committed after November 1, 1987. That does not mean that after a defendant is released from prison he is no longer under any supervision. The guidelines recommend that a court impose a term of "supervised release" whenever it sentences a defendant to more than a year in prison.[85] Terms of supervised release range from one to five years, and sometimes even life, depending on the offense and the maximum punishment.[86]

Defendants on supervised release are under the supervision of probation officers. They must report to their probation officers on a regular basis. They also need permission from their probation officers to travel outside of their district. Defendants on supervised release must follow numerous conditions, many of which are listed in USSG § 5D1.3. For example, defendants on supervised release must work unless their probation officers excuse them. They are also not allowed to be in touch with the people they met in prison, unless their probation officers allow it. Federal law allows a court to terminate a term of supervised release after a defendant has successfully completed one year of supervised release.[87]

A defendant who violates one of the conditions of supervised release can be sent to prison for up to the full term of supervised release. Before a court can send someone to prison for violating a term of supervised release, it must "consider" many of the same factors that it had to consider before imposing sentence in the first place.[88] Those factors include the sentencing guidelines and policy statements. Chapter Seven of the Guidelines Manual includes policy statements relevant to the revocation of supervised release. Whether a defendant who violates the conditions of supervised release will be sent to prison, and if so, for how long, depends on the seriousness of the violation. Defendants who violate supervised release are not usually sent to prison for the full term of the supervised release. How long a violator must serve depends on the seriousness of the violation and the violator's criminal history category. Chapter 7, part B of the guidelines deals with violations of probation and supervised release.

Fines, restitution, forfeitures, special assessments, and costs of incarceration.

Every federal sentence includes a $100 special assessment for each felony count of conviction.[89] For example, if a defendant is convicted on 10 felony counts, he will receive a $1,000 special assessment.[90] Sentences often include other financial penalties as well, such as restitution, fines, and forfeitures.

Restitution is an order to pay money that goes to the victims of the offense. Courts are often required to order defendants to pay the full amount of victims' loss as restitution. A court must order full restitution in most cases even if the defendant does not and never will have the money to pay it. If a defendant does not have resources to pay the restitution, the guidelines recommend that the court order him to make small monthly payments that he can afford.[91] A court can require a defendant to make payments on a restitution order as a condition of supervised release.

The guidelines recommend that a court impose a fine unless the defendant is unable to pay one and is unlikely to become able to pay one.[92] Courts do not impose fines in most cases, because most defendants are unable to pay them. The guidelines recommend a range for fines based on a defendant's offense level. A defendant's criminal history does not affect the fine range. For example the fine range for offense levels 16-17 is $5,000 to $50,000. The fine table is found at USSG § 5E1.2(c)(3). A court must consider this range, just as it must consider the guideline imprisonment range. But it is no more required to impose a fine within the range than it is to sentence within a range. If a court orders a defendant to pay restitution and a fine, any money the defendant pays will be used to pay the restitution first.

A few statutes require defendants to pay the cost of their prosecution. These include several tax offenses, as well as larceny or embezzlement in connection with commodity exchanges. These statutes are listed in the commentary which follows USSG § 5E1.5.

Finally, some statutes require a court to impose an order of forfeiture as part of the sentence. When property is forfeited, it is turned over to the government. Racketeering and drug laws, for example, require defendants to forfeit to the government certain property used in the offense or purchased with money gained from the offense.

Appeals from Sentencing Decisions

Prior to the guidelines, it was nearly impossible to appeal a sentence. That changed with the guidelines system. When the guidelines were mandatory, it was possible to appeal a sentence if it was imposed as a result of an incorrect application of the guidelines or if the court departed upwards. The government could also appeal sentences it believed were imposed as a result of an incorrect application of the guidelines or if the court departed downwards. After *Booker*, it is still possible for defendants and the government to appeal sentences. Now Courts of Appeal review sentences for "reasonableness."

There are two types of "reasonableness" which courts of appeals review. The first thing a court of appeals does is to review a sentence for procedural reasonableness. There are several factors an appeals court looks to to determine procedural reasonableness. First, it looks to whether the district court correctly calculated the guideline range. If the district court did not calculate the guideline range correctly, then it did not consider the correct range as required by § 3553(a). That makes the sentence procedurally "unreasonable." Appellate courts review guideline issues *de novo*. In a *"de novo"* review, the appeals court decides an issue from scratch.

The appeals court will also determine procedural reasonableness by looking at whether the district court considered the other § 3553(a) factors and the arguments of the parties for a sentence outside the guideline range. District courts must adequately articulate their reasons for imposing a particular sentence. If a court rejects an argument for a sentence outside the guideline range, it must adequately explain its reasoning. If it does not, the sentence is procedurally unreasonable.

Appeals courts also review sentences for substantive reasonableness. Although *Booker* promised that district court judges would finally be freed from the constraints of the guidelines and allowed to exercise their discretion to do justice at sentencing, appellate courts soon rejected numerous below-guideline sentences as "unreasonable" simply because they did not believe that the mitigating circumstances on which the district courts relied were significant enough to support large "variances" from the bottom of the guideline ranges. After the Supreme Court held that appellate courts (but not district courts) may presume that sentences within the advisory guideline range are "reasonable,"[93] the message seemed to be that while the guidelines were "advisory," district courts that didn't want to be reversed should not stray too far from the "advisory" range.[94] All that changed in December 2007, when the Supreme Court announced its decisions in *Gall v. United States*,[95] and *Kimbrough v. United States*,[96] opening up a new era in federal sentencing in which judges will once more be allowed to be judges.

Gall involved a conspiracy to distribute the illegal drug, "ecstasy." Although the guidelines recommended a sentence of 30-37 months' imprisonment, the district court sentenced Gall to 36 months' probation. The court cited several unusual mitigating factors to supports its sentence. First, Brian Gall committed his offense when he was an immature 21-year-old college sophomore, and an ecstasy user himself. Second, several months after joining the conspiracy, Gall voluntarily stopped using illegal drugs and formally notified other members of the conspiracy that he was withdrawing from it. After that, Gall not only never used or distributed any illegal drugs, he finished his education and went to work in the construction industry. After four years of leading an exemplary life, the government rewarded his rehabilitation with an indictment. Gall pled guilty. At sentencing, the court explained that a probationary sentence was sufficient, but not greater than necessary, to meet the goals of sentencing, because Gall had in essence rehabilitated himself some four years before he had even been indicted. The government appealed and the Eighth Circuit reversed, holding that the district court's "100%" variance from the guideline range was not supported by sufficiently extraordinary reasons. The Supreme Court reversed the Court of Appeals.

Although *Gall* noted that it is "uncontroversial that a major departure should be supported by a more significant justification than a minor one,"[97] the Court explicitly "reject[ed] an appellate rule that requires 'extraordinary' circumstances to justify a sentence outside the Guidelines range."[98] It also "reject[ed] the use of a rigid mathematical formula that uses the percentage of a departure as the standard for determining the strength of the justifications required for a specific sentence."[99] The Court noted that these approaches come perilously close to establishing a presumption that sentences outside the guideline range are "unreasonable" – a presumption the Court previously rejected in *Rita*. The Court was particularly critical of what it termed the "mathematical approach." Viewing variances as percentages of the bottom of the guideline range tend to make sentences of probation seem "extreme," since "a sentence of probation will always be a 100% departure regardless of whether the Guidelines range is 1 month or 100 years."[100] The Court was also critical of the fact that this approach also "gives no weight" to what the Court characterized as the "substantial restriction of freedom involved in a term of supervised release or probation,"[101] – a subtle invitation to courts to impose sentences of probation more often.

But *Gall* did more that invalidate particular approaches to reviewing variances from the guidelines. It reminded the Courts of Appeals that *Booker* not only invalidated the statutory provision that made the Guidelines mandatory (18 U.S.C. § 3553(b)(1)), it also invalidated 18 U.S.C. § 3742(e), which directed appellate courts to review departures from the Guidelines *de novo*. Prior to *Gall*, the Courts of Appeals seemed to ignore the significance of *Booker's* invalidation of § 3742(e). While the Supreme Court thought *Booker* had "made it . . . clear that the familiar abuse-of-discretion standard of review now applies to appellate review of sentencing decisions,"[102] the Court found that the decisions of the Courts of Appeals which required "extraordinary" reasons for significant deviations from the guidelines "more closely resembled *de novo* review."[103]

Gall makes it clear that the Supreme Court meant what it said in *Booker*: While sentencing courts must consider the guideline range as a "starting point," the "Guidelines are not the only consideration."[104] District courts must also consider *all* of the other factors listed in 18 U.S.C. § 3553(a). Once a Court of Appeals is satisfied that a district court has properly considered all of the factors listed in 18 U.S.C. § 3553(a), its review of a sentence is under the deferential abuse of discretion standard. While a Court of Appeals "may consider the extent of the deviation, [it] must give due deference to the district court's decision that the § 3553(a) factors, on a whole, justify the extent of the variance. The fact that the appellate court might reasonably have concluded that a different sentence was appropriate is insufficient to justify reversal of the district court."[105] *Gall* does not mean that a district court's non-guideline sentence cannot be reversed for substantive unreasonableness. But such reversals are likely to be uncommon.

While *Gall* held that a district court does not abuse its discretion by basing a below-guideline sentence on offender characteristics, *Kimbrough* held that a district court does not abuse that discretion when it bases a below-guideline sentence on disparities in sentencing caused by the guidelines themselves. In *Kimbrough*, the district court imposed a below-guideline sentence in a crack cocaine case, because it disagreed with the Sentencing Commission's and Congress's judgment that the distribution of any quantity of crack cocaine should be punished as severely as the distribution of one hundred times as much powder cocaine – the infamous "100 to 1 ratio."

The essence of the holding in *Kimbrough* is that a district court's judgment that a particular sentence is "sufficient, but not greater than necessary" (the overarching command of 18 U.S.C. § 3553(a)) is entitled to great weight, even if the district court's judgment is based in part on its disagreement with the policies behind the applicable guideline. *Kimbrough* gave defense attorneys license to think creatively about how guideline sentences themselves create "unwarranted disparities." It may now be entirely possible to obtain a lower non-guideline sentence by arguing among other reasons that a particular guideline sentence would create unwarranted disparities with sentences imposed in similar state cases. For example, the extremely harsh guidelines for simply downloading child pornography from the internet may be particularly vulnerable to attack after *Kimbrough*.

Although the promise of *Kimbrough* is great, it is important to remember that in many ways the history of the crack guideline makes it unique. While the majority observed that in the "ordinary" case, "the Commission's recommendation of a sentencing range will 'reflect a rough approximation of sentences that might achieve § 3553(a)'s objectives,'" it seemed to place special significance on the fact that the Sentencing Commission long ago concluded that the 100-to-1 ratio was unjust. It remains to be seen whether the broadest reading of *Kimbrough* will enable future challenges to overly harsh guidelines.

The pendulum has finally swung to the point that judges now have more discretion than they have ever had since pre-guideline days to fashion an appropriate sentence in a particular case. Now it's up to defense attorneys to present sentencing courts with the evidence and arguments they need to exercise that discretion to produce just sentences

Written plea agreements

Written plea agreements can help defendants receive lower sentences. There are several ways they can help. First, the government can agree to accept a plea to particular counts and to dismiss others. Sometimes this can reduce a defendant's guideline range. That is because the offense of conviction controls the selection of offense guideline. A government agreement to dismiss counts with higher offense levels can make a difference in the guideline range. The offense level for a count which charges selling drugs near a school is higher than the offense level for a regular drug count. A defendant could lower his guideline sentencing range (and potentially receive a lower sentence for that reason) by accepting a plea to counts which do not charge distribution near a school in exchange for the government dropping counts which do.

Sometimes a government agreement to drop counts makes no difference in the guideline range. For example, a government agreement to drop two counts of tax evasion in exchange for a plea to one count may make no difference in guideline range if they were all part of one scheme. The tax guideline measures the seriousness of the offense by the amount of the tax loss. Because of this, relevant conduct will require the court to use the entire loss under any scheme that was part of the offense of conviction. If the dismissed counts were part of the same scheme, they would be used to calculate the range for the count to which the defendant pled. A plea to one count of tax evasion might nevertheless be helpful, since in most cases it would put a five-year cap on any sentence. A defendant found guilty on three counts of tax evasion could theoretically receive anything up to a 15-year sentence.

In some plea agreements, the government and defendant agree specifically on the appropriate sentence. These are known at "C" pleas, after Rule 11(c)(1)(C) of the Federal Rules of Criminal Procedure. If a court accepts a "C" plea, it must impose the agreed-on sentence. If that sentence is less than the defendant would have likely received without it, then the agreement provides a valuable benefit.

Some plea agreements contain promises by the defendant to help the government investigate or prosecute other people. These parts of plea agreements are called "cooperation agreements." Cooperation agreements are discussed in the section on substantial assistance.

In other agreements, the government may agree to make or not to make certain recommendations, or the government and the defendant may stipulate to certain facts relevant to the calculation of the guidelines. Such recommendations and stipulations are not binding on the court. They nevertheless may provide valuable benefits. When the government and the defendant both agree, it is difficult for the court to do anything other than implement the agreement. Some stipulations can result in a higher offense level. This can happen if a stipulation specifically establishes that the defendant committed offenses other than the ones to which he agreed to plead guilty. When this happens, the guidelines require the court to calculate the guideline offense level as though the defendant had been convicted of the additional counts.[106]

Sometimes plea agreements place restrictions on the defendant. For example, some agreements require defendants to waive their rights to appeal. Others may require them to agree not to seek a downward departure, or not to contest certain upward adjustments. Before a defendant accepts such agreements, he should first consider the likely sentence he would receive if he were to plea guilty without an agreement. In some cases, the benefits of a written plea agreement are so small, that "pleading open" is the better option.

After sentencing – taking advantage of favorable guideline amendments

The guidelines which the court used at sentencing can change. Some amendments make the guidelines harsher. Once a defendant is sentenced, he is protected from that kind of change. Amendments can also reduce offense levels. Defendants who have already been sentenced can sometimes take advantage of these reductions. Before a defendant who has already been sentenced can take advantage of an amendment, the amendment must be listed in USSG § 1B1.10.

If an amendment is listed in § 1B1.10, the sentencing court has the discretion to modify a defendant's sentence. The sentencing court does not have to reduce a defendant's sentence based on a retroactive amendment. Once the guidelines make an amendment retroactive, the defendant may make a motion to modify sentence. The sentencing court could also modify the sentence on its own, without a motion.[107]

One of the most significant changes to the guidelines which was shortly thereafter made retroactive involved the "crack" cocaine guidelines.

On November 1, 2007, a new guideline amendment (Amendments 706 and 711) became effective that results in somewhat lower offense levels in many crack cocaine cases. Generally speaking, after November 1, offense levels in cases involving crack cocaine will be two levels lower than they would have been. The amendments make changes to the drug quantity table in USSG § 2D1.1(c) as well to Application Note 10 of that guideline.

These amendments are the culmination of a more than ten years' effort by the Sentencing Commission and sentencing reform groups to correct a serious pattern of unfairness in the sentencing of crack cocaine cases. The problem began when Congress passed the Anti-Drug Abuse Act of 1986. That law established mandatory minimum and statutory maximum sentenced based on drug quantities. It also established a 100-to-1 ratio between powder and crack cocaine. Under the law, 100 times as much powder cocaine was required to trigger a given mandatory minimum and statutory maximum when compared to the amount of crack cocaine required. The problem got even worse when the Commission adopted the same ratio in setting guideline offense levels in crack and powder cocaine cases.

By 1995, the Sentencing Commission had concluded that the 100-to-1 ratio was based on false presumptions. The Commission concluded that crack was not significantly more dangerous or harmful than powder, and therefore proposed amending the guidelines to eliminate the 100-to-1 ratio and to replace it with a 1-to-1 ratio. Congress rejected that amendment, but asked the Commission to propose changes to the law. The Commission did just that in 1997 and 2002, but Congress took no action. Finally, in 2007, the Commission proposed more modest changes to the crack-powder ratio, and congress allowed them to become effective on November 1, 2007. The mandatory minimum statutes, however, have not been altered.

While the change became effective on November 1, the Commission had not yet decided whether to make the amendment retroactive. If a guideline amendment that lowers offense levels is not made retroactive, then people sentenced to higher terms of imprisonment under the old rule do not benefit. Following public hearings on the retroactivity issue, the Commission unanimously decided on December 11, 2007, to make the amendments retroactive–but only beginning March 3, 2008.

What that means is that beginning March 3, 2008, a defendant already serving a sentence in a case involving crack cocaine will be able to apply to the sentencing court for a reduction in sentence. The Sentencing Commission estimates that over 19,500 inmates could be affected by this newly retroactive guideline.

The Sentencing Commission's decision to make the new crack guideline retroactive is a good thing, but it does not guarantee a lower sentence. When the Sentencing Commission makes a guideline retroactive, it gives the court the *power* to lower a sentence–but it does not *require* the court to lower it. Before deciding to lower a particular defendent's sentence, someone has to make a motion asking for the sentence to be modified. Then the court first has to consider the factors listed in 18 U.S.C.§ 3553(a). These are the same factors a court should have considered before imposing sentence in the first place, although in most of the 19,500 cases the factors most likely were given only limited consideration because the Guidelines were thought to be mandatory at the time before the case of *U.S. v. Booker* was decided. After *Booker*, this consideration can be much wider-ranging. Included among those factors are the history and characteristics of the defendant and the need to protect the public from further crimes of the defendant. If afer considering those factors, the Court believes that a lower sentence would be "sufficient, but not greater than necessary" to achieve the goals of sentencing, it may lower the defendant's sentence–but only "if such a reduction is consistent with applicable policy statements issued by the Sentencing Commission." 18 U.S.C. § 3582(c)(2).

This last requirement used to be satisfied simply by showing that the amendment is listed in USSG § 1B1.10(c) (p.s.) However, beginning March 3, 2008, the Sentencing Commission has added new requirements designed to reduce a court's discretion. This amended policy statement says that courts may not lower a sentence in cases where the amended guideline does not result in a lower guideline range. Even if the new range is lower, the policy statement attempts to prevent courts from imposing sentences lower than the bottom of the new range. The policy statement makes an exception for cases in which the court had previously departed downward. In such cases, the new sentence may be proportionally less than the new guideline range. The new policy statement also attempts to prevent courts from lowering sentences where defendant's already received lower non-guideline sentences pursuant to *United States v. Booker*, 543 U.S. 220 (2005). We believe that these new restrictions can be challenged, because they limit the discretion Congress intended to give courts in § 3582(c)(2).

Whether a particular defendant gets his or her sentence lowered will at minimum depend on whether the court is convinced that a lower sentence will be adequate to meet the goals of sentencing. Some defendants will need to present a sophisticated legal argument even to convince a judge that they are *eligible* for a reduction in sentence.

NOTES

1. 18 U.S.C. § 1341.

2. 18 U.S.C. § 1956.

3. 543 U.S. 220 (2005).

4. 18 U.S.C. § 3553(a).

5. 18 U.S.C. § 3553(a)(2).

6. 18 U.S.C. §§ 3553(a)(4) and (a)(5).

7. 18 U.S.C. § 3553(a)(1).

8. 18 U.S.C. § 3553(a)(2).

9. 18 U.S.C. § 3553(a)(3).

10. 18 U.S.C. § 3553(a)(6).

11. 18 U.S.C. § 3553(a)(7).

12. The Guidelines have been amended almost every year since they began in 1987. The version of the Guidelines in effect on November 1, 2007, is the one this booklet uses.

13. You can find the Sentencing Table at the back of this booklet at Appendix A.

14. USSG § 2C1.2.

15. USSG § 2C1.1.

16. *See* USSG § 1B1.3(a)(1).

17. USSG § 1B1.3(a)(2).

18. *Id.*

19. USSG § 1B1.11(a).

20. USSG § 1B1.11(b)(1).

21. USSG § 1B1.1(a).

22. USSG § 1B1.2(a).

23. USSG § 2B1.4(a).

24. USSG § 2S1.1(a)(1).

25. USSG § 2E1.1(a).

26. *See* USSG § 2B1.1(b)(1).

27. USSG § 2D1.1(b)(1).

28. USSG § 2D1.7(b)(1).

29. USSG § 2R1.1(c) and (d).

30. USSG § 2K2.4(d)(1).

31. USSG § 2M6.1(d)(1).

32. USSG § 1B1.1(c).

33. USSG § 3A1.1(b)(1).

34. USSG § 3A1.2.

35. USSG § 3A1.3.

36. USSG § 3A1.4.

37. USSG § 3B1.1.

38. USSG § 3B1.2.

39. USSG § 2D1.1(a)(3).

40. USSG § 3B1.3.

41. USSG § 3B1.4.

42. USSG § 3D1.4.

43. USSG § 3D1.2.

44. USSG § 3D1.2(d).

45. USSG § 3D1.2(b).

46. USSG § 3D1.3(a).

47. USSG § 3D1.2(c).

48. USSG § 3D1.3.

49. USSG § 3D1.4(a) and (b).

50. USSG § 3D1.4(c).

51. USSG § 1B1.1(e).

52. USSG § 3E1.1(a).

53. USSG § 3E1.1(b).

54. USSG § 3E1.1(b).

55. USSG § 4A1.1(a).

56. USSG § 4A1.1(b).

57. USSG § 4A1.1(c).

58. USSG § 4A1.1(d).

59. USSG § 4A1.1(e).

60. Now that the guidelines are no longer mandatory, there is no significant difference between a guideline and a guideline policy statement. A sentencing court must "consider" guidelines as well as guideline policy statements prior to imposing sentence.

61. When the guidelines were mandatory, a sentencing court was required to impose sentence within the sentencing guideline range, unless there was a basis on which to "depart." "Departures," and their significance under the advisory guidelines, are discussed on pages 21-25 of this Guidebook.

62. USSG § 5G1.1(a).

63. *See* USSG § 5G1.2(d).

64. USSG § 5G1.1(b).

65. 18 U.S.C. §§ 1111 (murder), 3559(c) ("three strikes").

66. USSG § 4B1.1.

67. 18 U.S.C. § 2247.

68. 21 U.S.C. § 841(b)(1)(B)(vii).

69. 18 U.S.C. § 3553(a)(4).

70. *Id.* § 3553(a)(1).

71. *Id.* § 3553(a)(2).

72. *Id.* § 3553(a)(3).

73. *Id.* § 3553(a)(5).

74. *Id.* § 3553(a)(6).

75. *Id.* § 3553(a)(7).

76. USSG § 5C1.2(a).

77. USSG § 2D1.1(b)(6).

78. USSG § 5C1.2(b).

79. USSG § 5B1.1(a)(1).

80. USSG § 5B1.1(a)(2).

81. USSG § 5C1.1(d)(2).

82. For an explanation of why a sentence of a year and a day results in less time that a year's sentence, see the practice tip on pages 52-53 of Chapter 2.

83. If the defendant is currently in custody serving another sentence, the Court must include special language in the judgment that will permit the new federal sent to run concurrent with the other sentence. Otherwise, the Bureau of Prisons will not begin to run the new federal sentence until the defendant has completed serving his other sentence.

84. USSG § 5G1.3(a).

85. USSG § 5D1.1(a).

86. USSG § 5D1.2.

87. 18 U.S.C. § 3583(e)(1).

88. 18 U.S.C. § 3583(e).

89. For offenses committed prior to April 24, 1996, the assessment is $50 for each count. 18 U.S.C. § 3013.

90. 18 U.S.C. § 3013.

91. USSG § 5E1.1(f).

92. USSG § 5E1.2(a).

93. *Rita v. United States,* 127 S.Ct. 2456 (2007).

94. Although a Court of Appeals may presume that a sentence within the guideline range is "reasonable," it may not presume that a sentence outside the range is "unreasonable."

95. 552 U.S. –, 128 S.Ct. 586 (Dec. 10, 2007).

96. 552 U.S. –, 128 S.Ct. 558 (Dec. 10, 2007).

97. *Id.* at 597.

98. 128 S.Ct. 595.

99. *Id.*

100. 128 S.Ct. 595.

101. *Id.* (internal citation omitted).

102. 128 S.Ct. at 594.

103. 128 S.Ct. at 600.

104. 128 S.Ct. 596.

105. 129 S.Ct. at 597.

106. USSG § 1B1.2(c).

107. *See* 18 U.S.C. § 3582(c)(2).

Chapter 2

Practice Tips

According to government statistics, approximately 94% of all federal criminal defendants plead guilty. Seventy-five percent of the remaining individuals who proceed to trial are convicted. There is therefore a 97% chance that a federal criminal defendant will face a sentencing judge. For most federal defendants "How much time am I going to do?" and "Where am I going to do it?" are key concerns. We offer the following tips to help attorneys and their clients obtain the lowest possible sentence to be served at the best possible facility under terms and conditions that will facilitate release at the earliest possible opportunity. These and other practice tips may also be found on our website: **www.alanellis.com**.

- After *Booker*, Courts of Appeals rejected numerous below-guideline sentences as "unreasonable" simply because they did not believe that the mitigating circumstances on which the district courts relied were significant enough to support large "variances" from the bottom of the guideline ranges. That changed with the Supreme Court's opinion in *Gall v. United States*.[1] In that case, the Court "reject[ed] an appellate rule that requires 'extraordinary' circumstances to justify a sentence outside the Guidelines range." The Court also "reject[ed] the use of a rigid mathematical formula that uses the percentage of a departure as the standard for determining the strength of the justifications required for a specific sentence." The Court made it clear that Courts of Appeals are not to impose their own judgment on what the appropriate sentence should be in any particular case. So long as the record demonstrates that district court considered the § 3553(a) factors and supported its sentence with a rationale that is supported by the record, the sentence should stand. It is therefore now more important than ever for defense attorneys to provide a rationale to the sentencing court.

The Court also makes clear that any attempt to give special weight to the sentencing guideline is contrary to its holding in *Booker*, which held the guidelines are advisory. See also, *Kimbrough v. United States*.[2] Both cases, decided the same day make it clear that the district courts are only required to give "some weight" to the advisory guidelines, as they are to the other 18 U.S.C. § 3553(a) factors.

Kimbrough goes one step beyond doing away with any special weight appellate courts have attached to the guidelines. It holds that a district court's judgment that a particular sentence is "sufficient, but not greater than necessary" is entitled to great weight, even if the district court's judgment is based in part on its disagreement with the policies behind the applicable guideline. Of particular note is the Court's holding that the district court in *Kimbrough* had properly imposed a below-guideline sentence to avoid the unwarranted disparity a guideline sentence would create between the defendant in that case, who was convicted on crack cocaine charges, and defendants convicted of powder cocaine offenses. *Kimbrough* gives defense attorneys license to think creatively about how guideline sentences themselves create "unwarranted disparities." It is now entirely possible to obtain a lower non-guideline sentence by arguing among other reasons that a particular guideline sentence would create unwarranted disparities with sentences imposed in similar state cases. For example, the extremely harsh guidelines for simply downloading child pornography from the internet may be particularly vulnerable to attack after *Kimbrough*.

- Accompany your client to probation officer meetings that are part of the Presentence Investigation Report (PSR) process. Since probation officers are overburdened, obtain in advance the forms and documents they need, and have your client complete and bring them to the initial interview. If you have any cases supporting your guideline position, highlight the relevant portions and bring them with you. Highlighted cases are more helpful to probation officers, who are not lawyers and are sometimes put off by memoranda of law.

- When you meet with the probation officer, find out his or her "dictation date." This is the date by which he or she must dictate the first draft of the PSR. When possible, it is extremely helpful to have the probation officer and the assistant U.S. attorney (AUSA) buy into what you believe is your client's offense behavior, role in the offense, and any grounds for downward departure before the dictation date. "Buying in" does not mean paying anybody off. It means getting them to agree that your position is not unreasonable. Remember that probation officers often have a psychological investment in their original draft PSR Since getting them to change a PSR can be difficult, put your effort into trying to get a good initial draft. That way, you won't have to file that many objections.

- Experience suggests that 80% of the time, a judge has a "tentative sentence" in mind even before the sentencing hearing begins. Unless you put on a tremendous dog-and-pony show at sentencing, it is likely that that "tentative sentence" is going to be your client's sentence. The best way to influence the judge's selection of "tentative sentence" is to file a sentencing memorandum approximately seven days before sentencing. If you can present the judge with character letters and a solid presentence memorandum that uses the § 3553(a) factors to demonstrate why a sentence below the guideline range is "sufficient, but not greater than necessary" to achieve the goals of sentencing, you will go a long way towards achieving the sentence you want.

- Prior to *Booker*, the only way to get a sentence below the guideline range was to use the guideline policy statements to show the court that there was a basis to "depart." Even after *Booker*, a court must "consider" guideline policy statements prior to imposing sentence. It is therefore still important to show, if you can, how the policy statements in Parts 5H and 5K call for a lower sentence. Even though a single mitigating factor may not warrant a downward departure, a combination of factors might.[3] Remember, a court can now impose a sentence below the guideline range even if there are no factors that would justify a "departure." Present the court with every mitigating factor you can think of. Even if you don't get a sentence below the guideline range, mitigating factors can often help in getting a sentence at the low end of the range. This is particularly important when the offense level and/or the criminal history score render high guidelines.

- Let judges be judges. *Booker* has altered the ground rules for justifying lower sentences. Be creative. Don't limit yourself to factors that would have supported downward departures under the guidelines. Think of things about your client and the offense that would make a sentence below the guideline range "sufficient" to meet the goals of sentencing, or else would make a sentence within the range "greater than necessary" to meet those goals.

- Even before *Booker*, departures based on the fact that the guidelines overstate the seriousness of the offense were sometimes recognized. See *United States v. Restrepo*, 936 F.2d 661 (2d Cir. 1991); *United*

States v. Alba, 933 F.3d 1117 (2d Cir. 1991); and *United States v. Lara*, 47 F.3d. 60 (2d Cir. 1994). Each of these cases supports the district court's granting of a downward departure beyond the four-level downward adjustment for a minimal role in the offense. Now, such arguments should always be considered.

- If your client is a cooperating witness, accompany him or her to any debriefings. Not only will you be able to clear up any future dispute as to what the client said, your presence will often facilitate the discussions, particularly if you've debriefed and prepped your client in advance.

- Many of us have been in the situation where even though our client has cooperated, the government has refused to file a 5K1.1 motion for downward departure based on substantial assistance. If you are ever faced with this unpleasant situation, either seek a downward departure based on "super/extraordinary acceptance of responsibility," or else argue that even without a 5K motion, the cooperation would make a lower sentence "sufficient," and a higher one "greater than necessary" to meet the goals of sentencing. If you inform the judge of your client's cooperation, you might persuade the judge to grant a downward departure or "variance" (which is what non-guideline sentences are sometimes called) and impose a sentence as low as it would have had the government filed a 5K1.1 motion. Remember, the "government motion requirement" of § 5K1.1 is only a guideline recommendation now. The judge must, of course, "consider" the policy statement that recommends that courts depart based on a defendant's substantial assistance only after the government has filed a 5K motion. For more information on maximizing the benefits of cooperation, take a look at the lead article in the Summer 2007 issues of *Federal Sentencing and Postconviction News*, our firm's quarterly newsletter, which can be found on the publications page of our website, **www.alanellis.com**.[4]

- Seek a "lateral" departure or "variance" that requires your client to serve the same amount of time as called for by the guidelines, but under more favorable conditions. For example, if the guidelines call for a 21-month sentence, ask the judge to depart downward or to grant a variance to a sentence of seven months of incarceration, followed by supervised release with a special condition that the client serve seven months in the correctional component of a community corrections center (CCC), considered the most onerous unit in a halfway house, followed by seven months of supervised release with home confinement and an appropriate amount of community service. Not only does this add up to the same 21 months that the client would normally serve, but it actually requires more time, since the client will not get good conduct time credit for either the community corrections center or home confinement portions of the sentence. While your client will serve the entire 21 months, the conditions of confinement will be better.

- Some judges don't like to recommend particular places of confinement at sentencing. Some believe that because they are not "correctional experts," they should not make any recommendation as to where a client should serve the sentence. Others are discouraged by letters they get from the Bureau of Prisons (BOP) advising them that their recommendations cannot be honored in a particular case. When the BOP fails to honor a judge's recommendation it is usually because the judge has recommended a facility incompatible with the defendant's security level. Although judicial recommendations are only recommendations, that does not mean they are not important. Not only does 18 U.S.C. § 3621(b)(4)(B) specifically contemplate these recommendations, but BOP Program Statement 5100.08 says that the Bureau welcomes a sentencing judge's recommendation and will do what it can to accommodate it. Bureau statistics show that in approximately 85% of the cases in which the defendant qualifies for the institution recommended by the judge, the court's recommendation is honored.

- Without a recommendation from the judge, prison overcrowding may prevent your client from being designated to the facility he prefers – even if he qualifies for it, and even if it is close to his home. Should there be only one slot open at a prison such as the Federal Prison Camp in Fairton, New Jersey, for example, and there are two defendants who want that placement, the one with the judicial recommendation is more likely to get it. If your judge is reluctant to make recommendations, it may help to get a copy of the Bureau's Program Statement 5100.08 and show the Court the page that deals with judicial recommendations.

- A year and a day sentence results in an inmate's serving approximately 47 days less than he would serve on a 12-month sentence because the 12-month sentence does not provide for good conduct time.[5]

- An inmate is generally not entitled to credit for time served on pre-trial release under home confinement or even in a halfway house as a condition of bond.[6]

- Certain considerations, termed Public Safety Factors by the BOP, will preclude camp placement even if an inmate is otherwise qualified for such placement. PSFs apply to defendants who are deportable aliens, high level/high volume drug traffickers, sexual offenders (including those convicted of child pornography offenses), defendants convicted of significant frauds that involved the use of a telephone, defendants with histories of juvenile violence, and defendants sentenced to terms of imprisonment of more than ten years. The Bureau of Prisons looks to the Presentence Investigation Report to determine the applicability of a particular Public Safety Factor.

- Generally, non-United States citizens are not eligible for federal prison camp placement. However, if U.S. Immigration and Customs Enforcement (ICE) or the Executive Office for Immigration Review (EOIR) determine that deportation proceedings are unwarranted, the offender may be eligible for Minimum security camp placement if otherwise qualified.

- The BOP's Residential Drug Abuse Program (RDAP).

    Pursuant to 18 U.S.C. § 3621(e) the Bureau of Prisons has implemented a nine month Residential Drug Abuse Program (RDAP) that can help an inmate receive up to a 12-month reduction in sentence and a six-month halfway house placement.

    Enrollment in RDAP is conditioned upon a diagnosis of substance abuse and independent verification in the prisoner's central file (usually the Presentence Investigation Report) that the inmate had a drug or alcohol problem within the year preceding confinement.[7] A prisoner without such verification is generally ineligible to participate.

    To be eligible for early release, a defendant must have been convicted of a non-violent offense.[8] The following categories of inmates are not eligible for early release, even if they successfully complete the drug treatment program:[9]

(i) INS detainees;
(ii) Pretrial inmates;
(iii) Contractual boarders (for example, D.C., State, or military inmates);
(iv) Inmates who have a prior felony or misdemeanor conviction for homicide, forcible rape, robbery, aggravated assault, or child sexual abuse offenses;
(v) Inmates who are not eligible for participation in a community-based program as determined by the warden on the basis of his or her professional discretion;
(vi) Inmates whose current offense is a felony:

(A) that has an element, the actual, attempted, or threatened use of physical force against the person or property of another, or
(B) that involved the carrying, possession, or use of a firearm or other dangerous weapon or explosive (including any explosive material or explosive device), or
(C) that by its nature or conduct, presents a serious potential risk of physical force against the person or property of another, or
(D) that by its nature or conduct involves sexual abuse offenses committed upon children.

An inmate must be eligible for community based program placement in order to fulfill the six-month halfway house (CCC) component of the RDAP. Otherwise, the inmate will not be able to obtain the up to 12-month reduction in sentence. The following inmates are ineligible for community-based program placement:

(i) Deportable aliens;
(ii) Inmates who require medical or psychiatric services;
(iii) Inmates who refuse to participate in the BOP Inmate Financial Responsibility Program;
(iv) Inmates expelled from the required drug abuse education course;
(v) Inmates with unresolved detainers or pending charges;
(vi) Inmates serving sentences of six months or less;

(vii) Inmates who pose a significant threat to the community as determined by the inmate's public safety factor, history of escape, repeated and serious institution rule violations, history of violence. NOTE: The BOP may consider the underlying conduct of prior convictions as described in the PSR, whether or not there was a conviction.

In addition to the requirements discussed above, inmates must also meet the following criteria:

(1) the inmate must have been sentenced pursuant to Title 18 U.S.C. Chapter 227, Subchapter D, under the Sentencing Reform Act (SRA), or under the "new law;"
(2) the inmate's prior adult criminal record includes no convictions which disqualify him/her for early release, based on the Director's Discretion; and
(3) the inmate has successfully completed all parts of the Bureau's residential drug abuse treatment program.

The possibility of the time reduction under § 3621(e) is an important factor in plea negotiations and sentencing. Charge bargaining can result in a better chance at RDAP eligibility (for example, by ensuring that the defendant is not convicted of a crime—such as a violent felony —which would preclude sentence reduction). Contesting a "gun bump," USSG § 2D1.1(b)(1), or the existence of a prior conviction for certain offenses can also increase a defendant's chances of receiving a sentence reduction for participating in RDAP. The Supreme Court has approved the BOP's exercise of discretion to deny early release to defendants with prior convictions for certain offenses, as well as to defendants who received an enhancement for possessing a gun.[10]

Judicial recommendations for RDAP and documentation of substance abuse in the Presentence Report help establish eligibility for treatment. The BOP requires that the inmate's substance abuse problem (including alcoholism) be substantiated in the presentence report to make him eligible to participate in residential treatment. A clear indication of a substance abuse problem in the presentence report which existed within one year of the defendant's incarceration and a sentencing court's recommendation that the defendant participate in residential treatment will help avoid problems of eligibility for early release.

The BOP's website at **http://www.bop.gov** offers updated lists of institutions offering residential drug abuse programs. For further information, also see Program Statement 5330.10.

- 18 U.S.C. § 3624(c) directs the BOP to ensure that prisoners spend "a reasonable part, not to exceed six months, of the last 10-percent[]" of his sentence in community placement, i.e., halfway house or home confinement. Inmate eligibility for community-based program placement has already been discussed in the Practice Tip concerning the BOP's Residential Drug Abuse Program (RDAP). Eligibility criteria for the six-month CCC component of the RDAP was also discussed in that Tip.

- Inmates can lose substantial credit towards their federal sentences because of the BOP's narrow interpretation of 18 U.S.C. § 3585(b), which governs credit for prior custody. The BOP interprets the statute to prohibit "double credit" in many instances for time served on a sentence imposed by different jurisdictions. For example, under BOP policy, any time credited toward another sentence (whether state or federal) prior to the imposition of the current federal sentence cannot be credited toward the new federal sentence, even if the earlier sentence resulted from related conduct, and even if the judge, whether state or federal, ordered the sentences to run concurrently.[11] The BOP's interpretation of § 3585(b) sometimes converts a concurrent sentence into a partially consecutive sentence regardless of the Judgment and Commitment Order, because the defendant will not begin getting federal credit until the court imposes the federal sentence.[12] There are ways to get around this, such as downward departures, adjustments under 5G1.3(b)(1), and the discretion courts have after *Booker*.

- Below guideline sentences are slowly on the rise. Unfortunately, so are above-guideline sentences. According to the statistics compiled by the U.S. Sentencing Commission since *Booker*, below guideline sentences have increased by over 7%, while above guideline sentences have increased by about 1%. This makes it important to hire a mitigation specialist if your client can afford it. Mitigation specialists are often social workers, former U.S. probation officers, or criminologists. Their training makes their interviewing technique more effective than that of most lawyers, and often allows them to obtain information a lawyer might not be able to get. For example, a forensic social worker with a background in psychiatric social work is better able than most lawyers to recognize when a client has a mental illness which may provide a ground for a downward departure based on diminished capacity. Mitigation specialists are also better able to identify unique family circumstances which may provide grounds for departure based on "extraordinary family circumstances." If you need a referral to a mitigation specialist, contact the author at 495 Miller Avenue, Suite 201, Mill Valley, California 94941 (Tel: 415-380-2550; Fax: 415-380-2550; Email: AELaw1@aol.com), or the National Association of Sentencing Advocates (202-628-2820), which has a listing of over 200 Mitigation Specialists throughout the country. Judges always want to know why the defendant committed the offense. Since mitigation specialists can help you answer the "why" question, they can often help you get the lowest possible sentence. We utilize the services of two mitigation specialists: Lianne C. Scherr, LCSW, a forensic psychiatric social worker, and Tess Lopez, a former federal probation officer. An interview with Ms. Lopez that was previously published in *Criminal Justice*, the journal of the Criminal Justice Section of the American Bar Association, is included at the back of this Guidebook. An interview with Ms Scherr that was published in the *Champion*, the journal of the National Association of Criminal Defense Lawyers, can be found on our website, www.alanells.com, under Criminal Justice Professional Profiles.[13]

- Remember the "safety valve."[14] A defendant who qualifies for the safety valve may receive a sentence below the mandatory minimum even if the government does not file a § 3553(e) motion. Qualifying defendants with offense levels of 26 or greater also receive an additional two-level decrease.[15]

- Be creative. Don't limit yourself to thinking about downward departures — but don't forget about them either. First think about the departures identified in the guidelines themselves. Then think of things that make your case unusual. If there are things that are unusual about your client or the offense — things that take the case outside the "heartland" of the guidelines, these can be good grounds for a departure. But don't stop there. After *Booker*, almost anything about your client, the offense, and the sentences that similarly situated defendants have received can support an argument that a sentence below the bottom of the guideline range is "sufficient, but not greater than necessary" to meet the goals of sentencing.

- The addition of one criminal history point may not change a defendant's Criminal History Category ("CHC"). But it can still be important to object to these seemingly harmless additions, and then to appeal if the district court denies the objection. Normally, a criminal history point that does not affect the sentencing range is "harmless error." But not always. In *United States v. Vargas*,[16] the Seventh Circuit remanded for resentencing based on a seemingly inconsequential criminal history point. The Court reasoned that the error was not "harmless," because it "might have affected" the district court's denial of the defendant's motion for downward departure based on the defendant's contention that his criminal history category significantly overrepresented the seriousness of his criminal history.[17] A single point might also affect prison designation, since the BOP now uses criminal history points to calculate an individual's security level.[18] Criminal History Points can affect the type of facility to which the offender may be assigned even if the judge sentences outside the guideline range after *Booker*.

NOTES

1. 552 U.S.__, 128 S. Ct. 586 (Dec. 10, 2007).

2. 552 U.S.__, 128 S.Ct. 558 (Dec. 10, 2007).

3. *See* USSG § 5K2.0 Commentary. 552 U.S.__, 128 S.Ct. 586 (Dec. 10, 2007).

4. http://www.alanellis.com/CM/Publications/newsletter-2007-summer. pdf. 552 U.S. ___, 128 S.Ct. 558 (Dec. 10, 2007) (allowing judges to impose lower sentences based on the unfairness of the 100 to 1 crack cocaine ratio).

5. 18 U.S.C. § 3624(b)(1).

6. *Reno v. Koray,* 515 U.S. 50 (1995).

7. Program Statement 5330.10.

8. The requirements an inmate must meet for early release are found in Program Statement 5330.10, Chapter 6. The term "non-violent offense" is defined in Program Statement 5162.04.

9. *See* BOP Program Statement 5330.10, Chapter 6, page 1.

10. *Lopez v. Davis,* 531 U.S. 230 (2001).

11. BOP Program Statement 5880.28.

12. Defendants held in custody prior to sentencing generally get credit for their time in custody prior to sentencing. But *not* if that prior custody was "credited against another sentence." 18 U.S.C. § 3585(b)

13. http://www.alanellis.com/CM/Publications/interview-with-lianne-scherr.asp.

14. 18 U.S.C. § 3553(f) and U.S.S.G. § 5C1.2.

15. USSG § 2D1.1(b)(4).

16. 230 F.3d 328 (7th Cir. 2000).

17. *See* USSG § 4A1.3 (p.s.).

18. *See* Program Statement 5100.08.

Appendix

SENTENCING TABLE
(in months of imprisonment)

	Offense Level	I (0 or 1)	II (2 or 3)	III (4, 5, 6)	IV (7, 8, 9)	V (10, 11, 12)	VI (13 or more)
		Criminal History Category (Criminal History Points)					
Zone A	1	0-6	0-6	0-6	0-6	0-6	0-6
	2	0-6	0-6	0-6	0-6	0-6	1-7
	3	0-6	0-6	0-6	0-6	2-8	3-9
	4	0-6	0-6	0-6	2-8	4-10	6-12
	5	0-6	0-6	1-7	4-10	6-12	9-15
	6	0-6	1-7	2-8	6-12	9-15	12-18
	7	0-6	2-8	4-10	8-14	12-18	15-21
	8	0-6	4-10	6-12	10-16	15-21	18-24
Zone B	9	4-10	6-12	8-14	12-18	18-24	21-27
Zone C	10	6-12	8-14	10-16	15-21	21-27	24-30
	11	8-14	10-16	12-18	18-24	24-30	27-33
	12	10-16	12-18	15-21	21-27	27-33	30-37
	13	12-18	15-21	18-24	24-30	30-37	33-41
	14	15-21	18-24	21-27	27-33	33-41	37-46
	15	18-24	21-27	24-30	30-37	37-46	41-51
	16	21-27	24-30	27-33	33-41	41-51	46-57
	17	24-30	27-33	30-37	37-46	46-57	51-63
	18	27-33	30-37	33-41	41-51	51-63	57-71
	19	30-37	33-41	37-46	46-57	57-71	63-78
	20	33-41	37-46	41-51	51-63	63-78	70-87
	21	37-46	41-51	46-57	57-71	70-87	77-96
	22	41-51	46-57	51-63	63-78	77-96	84-105
	23	46-57	51-63	57-71	70-87	84-105	92-115
	24	51-63	57-71	63-78	77-96	92-115	100-125
	25	57-71	63-78	70-87	84-105	100-125	110-137
	26	63-78	70-87	78-97	92-115	110-137	120-150
Zone D	27	70-87	78-97	87-108	100-125	120-150	130-162
	28	78-97	87-108	97-121	110-137	130-162	140-175
	29	87-108	97-121	108-135	121-151	140-175	151-188
	30	97-121	108-135	121-151	135-168	151-188	168-210
	31	108-135	121-151	135-168	151-188	168-210	188-235
	32	121-151	135-168	151-188	168-210	188-235	210-262
	33	135-168	151-188	168-210	188-235	210-262	235-293
	34	151-188	168-210	188-235	210-262	235-293	262-327
	35	168-210	188-235	210-262	235-293	262-327	292-365
	36	188-235	210-262	235-293	262-327	292-365	324-405
	37	210-262	235-293	262-327	292-365	324-405	360-life
	38	235-293	262-327	292-365	324-405	360-life	360-life
	39	262-327	292-365	324-405	360-life	360-life	360-life
	40	292-365	324-405	360-life	360-life	360-life	360-life
	41	324-405	360-life	360-life	360-life	360-life	360-life
	42	360-life	360-life	360-life	360-life	360-life	360-life
	43	life	life	life	life	life	life

REPRESENTING WHITE COLLAR CLIENTS IN A POST-BOOKER WORLD

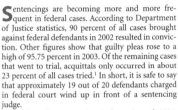

Sentencings are becoming more and more frequent in federal cases. According to Department of Justice statistics, 90 percent of all cases brought against federal defendants in 2002 resulted in conviction. Other figures show that guilty pleas rose to a high of 95.75 percent in 2003. Of the remaining cases that went to trial, acquittals only occurred in about 23 percent of all cases tried.[1] In short, it is safe to say that approximately 19 out of 20 defendants charged in federal court wind up in front of a sentencing judge.

Before the Sentencing Reform Act of 1984, which brought us the United States Sentencing Commission and the sentencing guidelines, defendants convicted of white collar crimes — tax evasion, fraud, antitrust offenses, insider trading, and embezzlement — could often expect to receive sentences of probation. The sentencing commission saw this as a "problem," which it "solved" with "guidelines that classify as serious many offenses for which probation previously was frequently given and provide for at least a short period of imprisonment in such cases."[2]

Short periods of confinement quickly rose to lengthy terms of incarceration. Then along came *Booker.*

United States v. Booker

On January 12, 2005, the Supreme Court handed down its decision in the consolidated cases of *United States v. Booker* and *United States v. Fanfan.*[3] *Booker* has two majority opinions — an opinion by Justice Stevens, which holds that the Federal Sentencing Guidelines, as interpreted in *Blakely v. Wash-*

ington,[4] violate the Sixth Amendment, and an opinion by Justice Breyer, which remedies that violation by striking language from the Sentencing Reform Act (SRA) that makes the guidelines mandatory.

Because the guidelines are now advisory, in cases sentenced after *Booker,* they are simply one factor among several that sentencing courts must consider in fashioning a sentence that is "sufficient but not greater than necessary" to achieve the purposes of sentencing set forth in 18 U.S.C. § 3553(a)(2).

Courts will still be required to "consider" the guideline range, as well as any bases for departure from that range, but they will no longer be *required* to impose sentence within that range — even where there is no basis to "depart." Under 18 U.S.C. § 3553(a), the key requirement is that the sentence in each case be "sufficient, but not greater than necessary:"

(A) To reflect the seriousness of the offense, to promote respect for the law, and to provide just punishment for the offense;

(B) To afford adequate deterrence to criminal conduct;

(C) To protect the public from further crimes of the defendant; and

(D) To provide the defendant with needed educational or vocational training, medical care, or other correctional treatment in the most effective manner.[5]

It is important to remember that when judges factor into a sentence the best way to provide defendants with needed rehabilitation, as required by § 3553(a)(2)(D), they are at the same time required to "recognize[e] that imprisonment is *not* an appropriate means of promoting correction and rehabilitation."[6] These four purposes can be summarized as retribution or "just desserts," deterrence (specific and general), incapacitation, and rehabilitation.

In determining whether the sentence is minimally sufficient to comply with the § 3553(a)(2) purposes of sentencing, the court must consider several factors listed in other subsections of § 3553(a). These factors are:

1. The nature and circumstances

By Alan Ellis and James H. Feldman, Jr.

of the offense and the history and characteristics of the defendant;

2. The kind of sentences available;
3. The [advisory] guidelines and policy statements issued by the sentencing commission;
4. The need to avoid unwarranted sentencing disparities among defendants with similar records who have been found guilty of similar conduct; and
5. The need to provide restitution to the victims of the offense.[7]

These directives often conflict with the kinds of sentences previously required by the guidelines, which in most cases offer no alternative to prison, even though in some cases, a defendant's education, treatment or medical needs may be better served by a sentence that permits the offender to remain in the community.

Title 18 U.S.C. § 3553(a)(7) directs courts to consider "the need to provide restitution to any victims of the offense." In many cases, imposing a sentence of no or only a short period of imprisonment will best accomplish this goal by allowing the defendant to work so that he can pay back the victim. Not only do the guidelines not permit this kind of creative sentence, they forbid departures to facilitate restitution.[8]

After *Booker,* courts are no longer bound by the departure methodology of the guidelines. Instead, a court may justify a sentence outside the calculated guideline range by factors that would not have previously permitted a departure from the guideline range. The *Booker* decision allows courts to consider factors that the guidelines previously precluded. In one of the earliest post-*Booker* decisions, Judge Lynn Adelman of the Eastern District of Wisconsin noted:

Under § 3553(a)(1) a sentencing court must consider the "history and characteristics of the defendant." But under the guidelines, courts are generally forbidden to consider the defendant's age, U.S.S.G. § 5H1.1, his education and vocational skills, § 5H1.2, his mental and emotional condition, § 5H1.3, his physical condition including drug or alcohol dependence, § 5H1.4, his employment record, § 5H1.5, his family ties and responsibilities, § 5H1.6, his socio-economic status, § 5H1.10, his civic and military contributions, § 5H1.11, and his lack of

guidance as a youth, §5H1.12. The guidelines' prohibition of considering these factors cannot be squared with the § 3553(a)(1) requirement that the court evaluate the "history and characteristics" of the defendant. The only aspect of a defendant's history that the guidelines permit courts to consider is criminal history. Thus, in cases in which a defendant's history and character are positive, consideration of all of the § 3553(a) factors might call for a sentence outside the guideline range.[9]

Judge Adelman concluded in that case that a sentence below the sentencing guidelines was justified. The defendant, a bank employee, had pleaded guilty to misapplication of bank funds by a bank officer. The defendant's guideline range was 37-46 months, after upward adjustments for loss, more than minimum planning, and abuse of position of trust. However, after considering all of the relevant factors, Judge Adelman imposed a sentence of one year and a day. In concluding that such a sentence was appropriate, Judge Adelman considered the defendant's motive for the offense, his responsibility for providing care of his elderly parents, and his history and character, which were exemplary before the offense conduct.

For the reasons cited by Judge Adelman, *Booker* will lead to more individualized sentencing, because now the sentencing guidelines are only one factor out of many that sentencing judges must consider. When courts had to impose sentence within the guideline range (barring a departure), they were limited to considering the factors listed by Judge Adelman to determine where in the range to impose sentence. It is now possible for courts to disagree with the judgment of the sentencing commission as to what the appropriate sentence should be.

After *Booker,* 18 U.S.C. § 3661 takes on new importance. That section provides that "no limitation shall be placed on the information concerning the background, character, and conduct of a person convicted of an offense which a court . . . may receive and consider for the purpose of imposing an appropriate sentence."

The sentencing commission has recently been urging judges, probation officers and attorneys to employ the following three-step methodology in imposing sentences:

STEP ONE: Calculate the now advisory guidelines according to old rules of the manual to arrive at a guideline range;

STEP TWO: Determine if a "departure" is warranted on the grounds authorized and addressed in the manual;

STEP THREE: Determine if a nonguideline sentence or "variance" is warranted under § 3553(a).[10]

Some judges have urged their colleagues to use this three-step process to demonstrate their adherence to the guideline process, even though it is only advisory, in an effort to persuade Congress not to tinker with law as it exists post-*Booker.*

With this in mind, here are some practice tips on how to obtain a lower sentence than called for by the advisory guidelines and any permitted departures.

First of all, do not acquiesce to the commission's suggested methodology. As far as the "advisory" guidelines are concerned, neither the statute itself nor *Booker* suggests that any one of the factors listed in 18 U.S.C. § 3553(a) (such as the sentencing range determined by the sentencing guidelines) is to be given greater weight than any other factor. Indeed, the guidelines and policy statements are only two of the many factors courts must consider.[11]

Practice Tips

• Answer the "why" questions. The most important two questions that you can answer for the sentencing judge is "why your client did what he did" and "why, if the judge takes a chance on him, he won't do it again."

• At the beginning of your sentencing memorandum, propose a sentence that you believe is "sufficient but not greater than necessary," and then go on to explain why.

• The United States Sentencing Commission has prepared a "post-*Booker*" manual for judges, probation officers, and attorneys. The commission advises judges to give "substantial weight" to the advisory guidelines. If the judge indicates that he or she is giving "substantial weight" to the sentencing guidelines, defense counsel should object on the ground that such a sentencing practice would make the guidelines as binding as they were before *Booker,* thus violating both the Sixth Amendment and the interpretation of Section 3553 adopted by the remedial majority in *Booker.* In the alternative, defense counsel should argue that since the "*weighted*" approach in effect makes the guidelines binding, thereby triggering Sixth Amendment protections, a court may use this approach to enhance a sentence only if it relies solely on facts proven to a jury beyond a reasonable doubt or admitted by the defendant. Even in cases in which a court has not indicated that it will give "substantial weight" to the guidelines, defense counsel should argue that the judge must base all guideline adjustments on facts proven beyond a reasonable doubt or, in the alternative, by clear and convincing evidence.

• Object to the presentence investigation report if it does not include all information relevant to Section 3553(a) purposes and factors.

• Use 18 U.S.C. § 3553(a) as a guide to structure your sentencing memorandum, but keep in mind that you are no longer bound by the sentencing guidelines. Where the facts support a traditional guidelines departure, argue for it. But when they don't, use the factors listed in 18 U.S.C. § 3553(a) to argue for a non-guideline sentence below the range. Remind the court that the guidelines are only one of seven equally important factors it must consider in determining a sentence that is "sufficient, but not greater than necessary, to comply with the purposes" of sentencing set forth in § 3553(a)(2).

• After *Booker*, district courts must still state reasons for the sentences they impose.[12] When that sentence is outside the guideline range, Section 3553(c)(2) still requires the court to explain in the judgment and commitment order why the sentence is outside the guideline range. When you argue for a sentence below the guideline range, prepare a written statement of reasons that the judge can adopt. Should the government appeal, a well-reasoned justification for the sentence can help ensure that it will meet the new test for "reasonableness."

• *Booker* has almost returned sentencing to pre-guideline days in which arguments that humanize a defendant and mitigate guilt can produce a sentence as low as probation (unless probation is precluded by law or unless a mandatory minimum applies). An important difference between pre-guideline sentencing and post-*Booker* sentencing is that a judge now must "consider" a list of seven factors (only one of which is the advisory guideline range) before imposing a sentence that is "sufficient but not greater than necessary" to achieve the purposes of sentencing set forth in 18 U.S.C. Section 3553(a)(2).

• Section 3553(a) requires a court to fashion a sentence that is "sufficient, but not greater than necessary" to achieve the goals of sentencing — one of which is to provide a defendant with the rehabilitation he needs.[13] At the same time, 18 U.S.C. § 3582(a) requires the court to "recognize [that] imprisonment is *not* an appropriate means of promoting correction or rehabilitation." (Emphasis added.) After *Booker*, it will therefore be possible in some cases to argue that these two requirements support a sentence without any term of imprisonment so as to meet a defendant's need for educational, vocational or medical services as part of his rehabilitation.

• Pre-*Booker*, the guidelines prohibited a court from relying on certain offender characteristics for downward departures.[14] Now that the guidelines are no longer mandatory, these limitations no longer restrict a court from imposing a sentence below the guideline range. Remember, not only does 18 U.S.C. § 3553(a)(1) *require* a court to "consider … the history and circumstances of the defendant," but § 3661 provides that "no limitation shall be placed on the information concerning the background, character and conduct of the defendant which a court may receive and consider for the purposes of imposing an appropriate sentence."

• *Booker* offers new opportunities to defendants who entered into pre-*Booker* plea agreements that preclude their seeking downward departures. Such defendants can seek non-guideline sentences or "variances" based on factors that would not previously have justified departures. In some cases, they may even be able to argue for lower sentences based on factors that may previously have justified departures.

• After *Booker*, a non-binding plea agreement that stipulates to the guideline calculation may still be helpful with a judge who has a strong inclination to follow the now-advisory guidelines. Plea agreements under Rule 11(c)(1) (C) that lock in a particular sentence or cap a sentence may now become more common as a way to restore some of the certainty to sentencing that was taken away by *Booker*.

• After *Booker*, the government has less leverage to force a defendant to waive the right to appeal or the right to seek a downward departure or a non-guideline sentence. The defense should now agree to such waivers only when the government gives it something substantial in exchange.

• After *Booker*, cooperation will remain an important way for defendants to earn lower sentences, but in cases without mandatory minimums, it will not be as critical for plea agreements to include a government promise to file a § 5K1.1 motion. A court may now impose a below-the-guidelines sentence based on a defendant's cooperation even without a government motion. In a case with a mandatory minimum, it will still be important to lock in a government's obligation to file a motion pursuant to 18 U.S.C. § 3553(e).

• In appropriate circumstances, considering that the zones in the guidelines are now also advisory, urge the court to impose a higher split sentence than was previously allowable under Zone C of the guidelines. For example, if the guidelines call for a 15-21 month range and you believe that a non-guideline sentence is appropriate, ask the sentencing judge to impose a sentence of eight months followed by supervised release with a special condition of seven months' home confinement.

• Moreover, if the opportunity presents itself, argue for probation or time served followed by supervised release with a special condition of eight months in a CCC (halfway house) followed by seven months of home confinement. Throw in some community service and you might wind up with a sentence that your client will be thrilled with.

• If you think your client is crazy, guess what? He may be crazy. Consider having him evaluated by a mental health professional, such as a psychiatrist, psychologist, or social worker. If there is evidence of head trauma, particularly head trauma that left your client unconscious, have him evaluated by a neuropsychologist, a mental health professional who specializes in brain injury. While a mental disorder may not rise to the level that would justify a diminished capacity downward departure under U.S.S.G. § 5K2.13, it still may be grounds for a lower sentence, either through a departure for extraordinary mental or emotional problems as suggested by U.S.S.G. § 5H1.3, or after taking into account the factors listed in 18 U.S.C. § 3553(a).

• Consider hiring a mitigation specialist. We have two in our firm, both of whom are forensic licensed clinical social workers. They are available to outside counsel. You can also contact the National Association of Sentencing Advocates, 514 Tenth Street, NW, Suite 1000, Washington, DC 20004, phone 202-628-0871, fax 202-628-1091, *www.sentencingproject.org/nasa*. Mitigation specialists, or sentencing advocates, as they are often called, develop individualized sentencing plans for attorneys whose clients face conviction and the prospect of incarceration. Defense attorneys use these individualized sentencing plans during plea negotiations to offer alternatives to lengthy incarceration to prosecutors, and during the pre-sentence phase and at sentencing to propose sentencing alternatives to probation officers and courts. Sentencing proposals typically focus on substance abuse and/or mental health treatment, victim restitution, community service, and the avoidance of future misconduct. By helping judges understand clients' life stories, they help attorneys argue, often successfully, for alternatives to lengthy incarceration.

• Read the following articles on sentencing, which can be found on our Web site (*www.alanellis.com*):

  a. *Baker's Dozen: Federal Sentencing Tips For The Experienced Advocate, Part I*
  b. *Baker's Dozen: Federal Sentencing Tips For The Experienced Advocate, Part II*
  c. *Answering The 'Why' Question: The Powerful Departure Grounds Of Diminished Capacity, Aberrant Behavior, And Post-Offense Rehabilitation*

• Read the following works on sentencing:

  a. Michael R. Levine, 108 MITIGATING FACTORS (May 1, 2005 ed.) (latest monthly update available from the author at 503-546-3927).
  b. BOOKER LITIGATION STRATEGIES MANUAL: A REFERENCE FOR CRIMINAL DEFENSE ATTORNEYS, Federal Defender's Office, Eastern District of Pennsylvania (April 20, 2005).

• Visit Sentencing Law and Policy blog, *http://sentencing.typepad.com*.
• Join the NACDL and BOPWATCH listservs. Nacdl.listserv@nacdl.org; *http://groups.yahoo.com/group/BOP-Watch/*.

Below The Guidelines Sentences

Mitigating factors justifying sentences below the advisory guideline range in white collar crime cases include, but are not limited to:

• **Collateral Consequences.** In *United States v. Gaind*,[15] a pre-*Booker* case, the Court reasoned that a sentence below the guideline range was justified based on the ways in which the defendant

had already been punished for his criminal conduct (he had been civilly prosecuted by the Office of the Comptroller and had to pay $75,000, suffered adverse publicity in a small town, ruined his business and suffered ill health and the death of his wife). The Court concluded that "the primary purposes of sentencing were partially achieved before the case was filed ... and [that the collateral punishment] partially satisfied the need for just punishment."

• **Out-of-Character Conduct.** Factors that can now justify a lower sentence in any case include: (1) a defendant's behavior that is a marked departure from the past, (2) an absence of pecuniary gain, (3) prior charitable and good deeds, (4) efforts to mitigate the effects of the crime, (5) long-term employment coupled possibly with recent unemployment, (6) an absence of prior criminal conduct, (7) the unlikelihood that the defendant will repeat the criminal conduct, (8) the defendant's motivation for committing the crime, (9) the conditions under which the defendant was operating when he committed the offense, such as the pressure of losing a job,

(10) psychological disorders that defendant was suffering from when he committed the offense. Support this basis for a lower sentence with letters from friends and family that express shock at defendant's atypical, out-of-character behavior.

• **A Defendant Is Able To Make Restitution If No Imprisonment Is Imposed.** Title 18 U.S.C. § 3553(a)(7) requires the sentencing court to consider the need to provide restitution to any victims of the offense. For crimes committed after October 27, 2003, the guidelines prohibited departures based on defendant's fulfilling a restitution obligation.[16] Not only does this prohibition lose its bite after *Booker*, but the requirement found in § 3553(a)(7) that the court take the need to provide restitution into account in fashioning sentences means that when a defendant's ability to pay restitution hinges on his continued ability to work, defense counsel may be able to convince the court not to impose any incarceration. Similarly, when defendants have already paid restitution, defense counsel may once more cite that fact to argue for lower sentences.

• **The Defendant's Age.** In *United States v. Nellum*,[17] a judge imposed a sentence below the guideline range on a 57-year-old defendant, because a sentence within the guideline range would mean that the defendant would be over the age of 70 at his release. The court found that the likelihood of recidivism for a man his age was very low citing a May 2004 government study. Consider arguing also, as a mitigating factor, that elderly inmates are more vulnerable to abuse and deprecation, have difficulty in establishing social relationships with younger inmates, and sometimes need special physical accommodations in a relatively inflexible physical environment. Moreover, first-time offenders are "easy prey for more experienced predatory inmates."[18]

• **Super Or Extraordinary Acceptance Of Responsibility.** For crimes committed on or after October 27, 2003, the guidelines eliminate this basis for departure. U.S.S.G. § 5K2.0(p)(2). Post-*Booker*, however, this is a mitigating factor and can be a ground for a below-the-guideline sentence. Super acceptance of responsibility can be based on post-offense restitution,[19] admission of guilt or other crimes about which government had no knowledge,[20] and forbearance of defenses to meritorious claims.[21]

• **Post-Offense Rehabilitation.**[22]

• **Post-Sentence Rehabilitation.** For crimes committed on or after November 1, 2000, U.S.S.G. §5K2.19 prohibits downward departures for post-sentencing rehabilitative efforts even if exceptional. Post-*Booker*, post-sentencing rehabilitation is a mitigating basis for a below-the-guidelines sentence at a resentencing following a reversal of defendant's conviction and/or sentence.

• **Extraordinary Family Circumstances.** For crimes committed on or after October 27, 2003, U.S.S.G. § 5H1.6 makes it more difficult to obtain a departure based on family ties or responsibilities. Post-*Booker*, extraordinary family circumstances or responsibilities, especially where incarceration will have a deleterious effect on innocent family members, can be a basis for a below-the-guideline sentence.

• **Defendant's Incarceration Would Cause A Loss Of Jobs Of Innocent Employees.** Because a small business will always be harmed whenever the owner is convicted of an offense and imprisoned, courts have generally not departed downward based on harm to innocent employees, except in extraordinary cases.[23] Post-*Booker*, however, this can be a strong argument for a below-the-guideline sentence.

• **Diminished Capacity.** For crimes committed after October 27, 2003, U.S.S.G. § 5K2.13 requires that diminished capacity must have "contributed substantially" as opposed to "significantly" to the commission of the offense. In light of *Booker*, even if an offender does not meet the criteria for a U.S.S.G. § 5K2.13 departure, his mental state may nonetheless be a basis for a below-the-guideline sentence.

• **Drug Or Alcohol Dependence Or Abuse — Gambling Addiction.** For crimes committed on or after October 27, 2003, the guidelines prohibit a departure on these grounds. *Booker* changes this result.

• **Other Factors.** For an exhaustive list of mitigating factors, see Michael R. Levine's "108 Mitigating Factors." [The latest monthly update is available from the author at 503-546-3927.]

Guideline Calculation

After *Booker*, courts will still calculate a defendant's guideline range in much the way as they did before *Blakely*. Judges will determine the offense level using the application principles established by the guidelines. As before, they will select the offense guideline based on the offense of conviction and will make other guideline decisions using "relevant conduct." Courts will probably still make factual determinations using the preponderance of the evidence standard although, arguably, they should be held to a higher standard such as "clear and convincing" evidence or even "beyond a reasonable doubt."[24]

Because the guidelines for economic crimes are driven by monetary factors, the first challenge defense attorneys face is to ensure that those figures are accurately calculated. For example, defense counsel must first make sure that the figure proposed by the presentence investigation report does not count the same money twice.

In some fraud cases, a defendant may supply a victim with a good or service — albeit not of the quality promised. Although the loss used to calculate the guideline offense level is generally reduced by the value of the good or service provided,[25] there are several exceptions to this rule. The guidelines now provide that no credit be given in two situations: (1) where a defendant falsely posed as a licensed professional, and (2) where the defendant falsely represented that the goods provided had received approval under a government regulatory scheme.[26]

Just as there are fraud cases in which victims receive something of value, there are also fraud cases in which defendants have no intent to cause financial loss to anyone. For example, a defendant may lie about his debts to obtain a loan that he fully intends to repay. If the defendant then defaults after repaying a portion of the debt, the loss under § 2B1.1 is *necessarily* the loss the victims actually sustain, since there is no intended loss. This is significant, because the guidelines provide that if the loss a defendant *intends* to inflict is greater than the loss his victims actually sustain, the sentencing court is to consider the intended loss in setting the offense level.[27] If a defendant who intends no loss had pledged assets to secure the debt, then the loss is reduced by the value of those assets.[28] The Ninth Circuit has held that this application note does not apply when intended loss is greater than actual loss.[29]

Where defendants *intend* loss, then the intended loss is used if it is greater than the actual loss.[30] It is important to remember that "intended" loss is not the same thing as "possible" loss. In *United States v. Titchell*,[31] the district court found an "intended" loss of over $17 million, because the defendant sent out 119,575 fraudulent invoices billing over $17 million. The court of appeals reversed, because the defendant "intended" the loss to be only $647,000, since when the defendant developed the scheme, he understood that a 3 percent return was the norm.

In the past, courts have differed on how to apply the intended versus actual loss principle in Ponzi schemes, where defendants do not *intend* for all victims to lose money. In a Ponzi scheme, the defendant deceives his victims into "investing" money, which the defendant steals, rather than invests. Defendants in such cases will often use "investments" by later victims to pay "profits" to earlier ones. This practice helps keep the scheme going by making it appear that the "investments" are producing significant returns for investors.

In the past, some courts reduced the loss by the money the defendant paid to some victims — other courts did not.

The Sentencing Commission resolved this conflict in November 2001 by amending U.S.S.G. § 2B1.1, Appl. Note 3(F)(iv), to provide that money paid to victims as part of the scheme may reduce loss — but only to the point that a victim is repaid money he or she had previously "invested." The guidelines do not reduce loss by the "profits" made by some victims, because those "profits" do not reduce the loss to any victim.

Defense counsel in fraud cases also need to ensure that losses that were not caused by the fraud do not affect the guideline offense level. For example, in *United States v. Rothwell*,[32] although the defendant's fraud caused the Small Business Administration to pay him progress payments on a disaster relief loan, the fraud did not cause any loss to the bank. That loss was caused by the defendant's lack of funds. In *United States v. Randall*,[33] a bankruptcy fraud case, HUD and the VA lost money when they foreclosed on properties whose mortgages they insured. Although the district court included these losses in the guideline calculus, the court of appeals reversed, because they were not caused by the defendant's fraud (*i.e.*, her lying about her name, social security number, and prior bankruptcies). The court found that the agencies would have incurred the same losses even without the bankruptcy fraud.[34]

The guidelines provide for upward adjustments under certain circumstances when the offense affects a "financial institution."[35] Whenever a presentence report attempts to apply one of these adjustments, defense counsel need to determine whether the institution involved qualifies as a "financial institution" as that term is defined in U.S.S.G. § 2B1.1, Application Note 1. In *United States v. Miles*,[36] for example, the court of appeals reversed the sentence in a Medicare fraud case, because Medicare is not a "financial institution."

In general, only losses to victims that are directly caused by fraud are included in loss. Consequential damages, such as "[i]nterest of any kind, finance charges, late fees, penalties, amounts based on agreed-upon return or rate of return, or other similar costs,"[37] are not included.[38] In *United States v. Izydore*,[39] the Court of Appeals held that a $210,158 bankruptcy trustee's fee should not have been included in loss, because although it was a consequence of the defendant's fraud, it was not money "taken" by the defendant.[40] If the interest, finance charge, late fee, or penalty is "substan-tial," U.S.S.G. § 2B1.1, Appl. Note 19(a)(*iii*) suggests that it could be a basis for an *upward* departure.

A similar principle applies in tax cases, where "tax loss does not include interest or penalties, except in willful evasion of payment cases under 26 U.S.C. § 7201 and willful failure to pay cases under 26 U.S.C. § 7203."[41]

The guidelines handle price-fixing cases somewhat differently. The offense level in such cases is not controlled by "loss," but by "volume of commerce," *i.e.*, sales made as part of the price-fixing scheme. Significantly, the guidelines limit the application of relevant conduct in price-fixing cases, by providing that:

> For purposes of this guideline, the volume of commerce attributable to an individual participant in a conspiracy is the volume of commerce done by him or his principal in goods or services that were affected by the violation.[42]

This limitation of the "relevant conduct" principle of U.S.S.G. § 1B1.3 is important, since without it, a defendant would also be responsible for the volume of commerce attributable to other companies involved in the price-fixing (so long as they were "reasonably foreseeable [and] in furtherance of the jointly undertaken criminal activity," and met the other criteria of U.S.S.G. § 1B1.3.[43]

A more contentious question in price-fixing cases is whether all sales during the period of price-fixing are included in the "volume of commerce." The Sixth Circuit held in *United States v. Hayter Oil Co.*[44] that they are, regardless of whether the sales were at or below the fixed price. Although *Hayter Oil* has been criticized,[45] at least one other court has followed the Sixth Circuit's lead.[46] The Second Circuit broke ranks with the Sixth Circuit, holding in *United States v. SKW Metals & Alloys, Inc.*,[47] that the government must prove that sales were in some way "affected" by the price-fixing scheme before they may be included in the volume of commerce. The court of appeals nevertheless granted the government's appeal and remanded for resentencing, because the district court had excluded *all* sales below the fixed price.[48] The court of appeals disapproved of this finding, reasoning that some sales below the fixed price could nevertheless have been "affected" by the scheme.

Departures

While courts have departed down-ward in white collar cases for the same "offender-related" reasons they depart downward in other cases, other mitigating "offense related" circumstances are unique to white collar offenses. For examples of "offender-related" departures, *see* Alan Ellis, *Let Judges be Judges! Downward Departures After Koon* (pts. 1-7), CRIMINAL JUSTICE (Winter 1998 through Summer 1999).

The theft/fraud guideline suggests the appropriateness of a downward departure in "cases in which the offense level determined under this guideline substantially overstates the seriousness of the offense."[49]

Downward Departures Have Also Been Granted Where:

- the defendant did not profit personally from his fraud.[50]
- the defendant had a good faith belief that his conduct was lawful.[51]
- the defendant's business would fold and his innocent employees suffer if he were imprisoned.[52]
- it was improbable that the scheme would succeed.[53]

In a wage tax withholding case, the First Circuit acknowledged that the district court could depart downward based on the defendant's intent to pay the withholding tax once his business became stable, but remanded for resentencing and for the district court to consider the concerns of the court of appeals with respect to the extent of the lower court's previous departure.[54] The court also held that unlike in fraud cases, multiple causes for the extent of loss in a tax case are not a basis for departure. In a tax evasion case, the Third Circuit has approved a departure based on prosecutorial manipulation of the indictment where the tax evasion was incidental to the underlying embezzlement case and the sentencing court found it was unusual for the government to charge tax evasion in addition to embezzlement in such a case.[55]

The guidelines for white collar crime are harsh, but solid investigation, creative thinking, and persuasive advocacy can often be combined to protect our clients from overly severe and excessive punishment.

Notes

1. Annual Report of the Administrative Office of the U.S. Courts (Statistical Years 1996-2003).

2. U.S.S.G. Ch. 1 Pt. A § 4(d).

3. 543 U.S. –, 125 S.Ct. 738, 160 L.Ed.2d 621 (Jan. 12, 2005).

4. 542 U.S. 296 (2004).

5. 18 U.S.C. § 3553(a)(2).

6. 18 U.S.C. § 3582(a).

7. At least one court has characterized these factors as taking into account the nature of the offense, the history and character of the defendant, and the needs of the public and any victims of the crime. See United States v. Galvez-Barrios, 355 F.Supp.2d 958, 960 (E.D.Wis. 2005).

8. See United States v. Seacott, 15 F.3d 1380, 1388-89 (7th Cir. 1994).

9. United States v. Ranum, 353 F.Supp.2d 984 (E.D. Wis. 2005).

10. The commission uses the term "variance" to mean a sentence below the otherwise applicable guideline range which cannot be justified as a "departure."

11. See United States v. Booker, 125 S.Ct. 764-65 (noting that the guideline range is only one of many factors a sentencing court must consider in determining a sentence).

12. 18 U.S.C. § 3553(c). See United States v. Webb, 403 F.3d 373, 385 n. 8 (6th Cir. 2005).

13. 18 U.S.C. § 3553(a)(2)(D).

14. See U.S.S.G §§ 5H1.4 (drug and alcohol abuse), and 5H1.12 (lack of youthful

guidance or a disadvantaged upbringing). Courts were prohibited from relying on other factors, except in extraordinary circumstances. See U.S.S.G. §§ 5H1.1 (age), 5H1.2 (education and vocational skills), 5H1.3 (mental and emotional conditions), 5H1.4 (physical condition and appearance), 5H1.5 (employment record), 5H1.6 (family ties and responsibilities), and 5H1.11 (charitable acts).

15. 829 F.Supp. 669 (S.D.N.Y. 1993), aff'd. 31 F.3d 73 (2nd Cir. 1994).

16. U.S.S.G. § 5K2.0(d)(5).

17. 2005 WL 300073 (E.D. Ind. Feb. 3, 2005).

18. Correctional Health Care Addresses the Needs of Elderly and the Chronically Ill and Terminally Ill Inmates, U.S Department of Justice, National Institute of Corrections, 2004 edition, pp. 9-10. It should be noted that throughout the report, the elderly are defined as age 50 or older.

19. United States v. Kim, 364 F.3d 1235 (11th Cir. 2004).

20. United States v. Demonie, 25 F.3d 343, 349 (6th Cir. 1994).

21. United States v. Faulks, 143 F.3d 133 (3d. Cir. 1998).

22. See, e.g., United States v. Sally, 116 F.3d 76, 82, (3d Cir. 1997) ("defendant achieves real gains in rehabilitating himself and changing his behavior"); United States v. Maddalena, 893 F.2d 815, 818 (6th Cir. 1989) (holding that district judge may consider defendant's "efforts to stay away from drugs as a basis for departing from the guidelines"); United States v. DeShon, 183 F.3d 888, 889-90 (8th Cir. 1999) (district court did not abuse its discretion in departing based on the defendant's extraordinary post-offense rehabilitation, evidenced by his renewed church life, acceptance of responsibility, hard work and diligence, strengthened family relationships, and participation in counseling); United States v. Jones, 158 F.3d 492, 503 (10th Cir. 1998) (district court did not abuse its discretion in departing downward based on defendant's post-offense rehabilitation evidenced by his regular work, counseling, and support of his children).

23. See United States v. Milikowsky, 65 F.3d 4 (2nd Cir. 1995) (finding extraordinary circumstances, Court affirms departure based on harm to innocent employees); cf. United States v. Olbres. 99 F.3d 28 (1st Cir. 1996) (remanding for district court to consider whether extraordinary circumstances exist to support departure based on harm to innocent employees; United States v. Sharapan, 13 F.3d 781 (3d Cir. 1994) (reversing departure — no extraordinary circumstances); United States v. Mogel, 956 F.2d 1555 (11th Cir.) (business ownership not basis for departure) cert. denied, 506 U.S.

857 (1992); United States v. Rutana, 932 F.2d 1155 (6th Cir.) (reversing departure — no extraordinary circumstances), cert. denied, 502 U.S. 907 (1991).

24. See United States v. Johansson, 249 F.3d 848, 853-54 (9th Cir. 2001) (clear and convincing standard); United States v. Thomas, 355 F.3d 1191, 1202 (9th Cir. 2004) (reasonable doubt). See also United States v. Huerta-Rodriguez, 355 F.Supp.2d 1019, 1928 (D. Neb. Feb. 1, 2005) ("it can never be 'reasonable' to base any significant increase in a defendant's sentence on facts that have not been proven beyond a reasonable doubt"); United States v. Ochoa-Suarez, 2005 WL 287400, 2005 U.S. Dist. LEXIS 1667 (S.D.N.Y. Feb. 7, 2005) (rejecting leadership adjustment, because no finding beyond a reasonable doubt by a jury that defendant qualified as a manager or supervisor under U.S.S.G. § 3B1.1).

25. See U.S.S.G § 2B1.1, Appl. Note 3(E)(i). See also United States v. Bolden, 325 F.3d 471 (4th Cir. 2003) (loss in Medicare fraud case did not include payments for legitimate services); United States v. Renick, 273 F.3d 1009 (11th Cir. 2003) (loss in CHAMPUS case which involved legitimate as well as fraudulent billing may not be determined by arbitrary estimate of fraudulent portion); United States v. Silver, 245 F.3d 1075 (9th Cir. 2001) (DoD defrauded when defendant provided generic parts instead of name brand parts as required by contract — loss reduced by value of generic parts even though the DoD threw them out); United States v. Hayes, 242 F.3d 1144 (3d Cir. 2001) (defendant hired as social worker after she forged her qualifications — loss was the salary she received, less the value of the services she provided); United States v. Fiorillo, 186 F.3d 1136 (9th Cir. 1999) (per curiam) (loss does not include price paid by victim for disposal of hazardous waste, which defendant properly handled); United States v. Sublett, 124 F.3d 693 (5th Cir. 1997) (loss does not include value of counseling provided by qualified counselors); United States v. Parsons, 109 F.3d 1002 (4th Cir. 1997) (legitimate expense reimbursement requests not included in loss); United States v. Alburg, 818 F.Supp. 1306 (N.D. Cal. 1993) (loss reduced by value of work performed).

26. See U.S.S.G § 2B1.1, Appl. Note 3(F)(v).

27. U.S.S.G § 2B1.1, Appl. Note 3(A).

28. U.S.S.G .§ 2B2.2, Appl. Note 3(E)(ii). See United States v. Henderson, 19 F.3d 917, 927-28 (5th Cir. 1994) (applying this principle); United States v. Kopp, 951 F.2d 521 (3d Cir. 1991) (same). United States v. Wells, 127 F.3d 739 (8th Cir. 1997) (loss reduced by value of future payments to bank on leases assigned as collateral); United States v. Downs, 123 F.3d 637 (7th Cir. 1997) (loss

reduced by value of assets pledged).

29. United States v. McCormac, 309 F.3d 623, 627-28 (9th Cir. 2002) (where defendant did not intend to repay loan, loss is not reduced by value of collateral).

30. U.S.S.G § 2B1.1, Appl. Note 3(A).

31. 261 F.3d 348 (3d Cir. 2001).

32. 387 F.3d 579 (6th Cir. 2004).

33. 157 F.3d 328 (5th Cir. 1998).

34. See also United States v. Daddona, 34 F.3d 163 (3d Cir. 1994) (where defendant, a registered agent of Employers Insurance of Wausau, did not purchase construction bond as promised, loss was not cost of completing failed project, since fraud did not cause project to fail; loss was money insurance company was required to pay); United States v. Marlatt, 24 F.3d 1005 (7th Cir. 1994) (where defendant misrepresented that he had clear title to condominiums, loss was cost to clear title, not unrelated reduction in value of condominiums); United States v. Stanley, 12 F.3d 17 (2d Cir. 1993) (although defendant used fraudulent mailing to induce purchases of overpriced bonds, people who did not receive the mailing also bought bonds; court excluded losses incurred by the latter group from guideline calculation).

35. See U.S.S.G § 2B1,1(b)(13).

36. 360 F.3d 472 (5th Cir. 2004).

37. U.S.S.G § 2B1.1, Appl. Note 3(D)(i).

38. See United States v. Seward, 272 F.3d 831 (7th Cir. 2001) (attorneys and executor's fees not included in loss in fraud against an estate).

39. 167 F.3d 213, 223 (5th Cir. 1999).

40. See also United States v. Sablan, 92 F.3d 865 (9th Cir. 1996) (value of bank employees' time spent meeting with FBI and each other to discuss offense is consequential loss not included in guideline calculation).

41. U.S.S.G § 2T1.1, Appl. Note 1. See United States v. Hopper, 177 F.3d 824, 832 (9th Cir. 1999) (applying this principle); United States v. Pollen, 978 F.2d 78, 91 n.29 (3d Cir. 1992) (criticizing, but applying rule in evasion of collection case).

42. U.S.S.G § 2R1.1(b)(2).

43. See United States v. Heffernan, 43 F.3d 1144, 1147 (7th Cir. 1994) (applying this principle).

44. 51 F.3d 1265 (6th Cir. 1995).

45. See Henry D. Fincher, Fining the Market: The Bumbling Price-Fixer and the Antitrust Guideline, 8 FED.SENT.REP. 244 (1996).

46. See, e.g., United States v. Andreas, 1999 WL 51806 (N.D. Ill, Jan. 27, 1999).

47. 195 F.3d 83 (2d Cir. 1999).

48. See United States v. SKW Metals & Alloys, Inc., 4 F.Supp.2d 166 (W.D.N.Y. 1997).

49. U.S.S.G § 2B1.1, Appl. Note 19(C). See, e.g., United States v, McBride, 362 F.3d

360 (6th Cir. 2004) (although intended loss drives offense level even where scheme to defraud could not have succeeded, impossibility of scheme can be a basis for departure); United States v. Lauersen, 348 F.3d 329 (2d Cir. 2003) (where multiple adjustments result in very high offense level that substantially overstates seriousness of offense, district court may depart downward); United States v. Kushner, 305 F.3d 194 (3d Cir. 2002) (remanded to consider departure where defendant voluntarily turned in preprinted checks with a face value of $455,203.99); United States v. Gregorio, 956 F.2d 341 (1st Cir. 1992) (downward departure appropriate where degree of loss was caused by downturn in economy); United States v. Graham, 146 F.3d 6 (1st Cir. 1998) (loss overstates culpability where lower loss attributed to similarly situated defendants); United States v. Monaco, 23 F.3d 793 (3d Cir. 1994) (loss overstates seriousness where defendant had no intent to steal); United States v. Stuart, 22 F.3d 76 (3d Cir. 1994) (affirming loss calculation based on face value of stolen bonds, but suggesting appropriateness of departure on remand where defendant received little money for participation in offense, causing loss to overstate seriousness of offense).

50. See, e.g., United States v. Broderson, 67 F.3d 452 (2d Cir. 1995).

51. See, e.g., United States v. Jasin, 25 F.Supp.2d 551 (E.D.Pa. 1998), aff'd, 191 F.3d 446 (3d Cir. 1999) (table).

52. See, e.g., United States v. Olberes, 99 F.3d 28 (1st Cir. 1996); United States v. Milikowsky, 65 F.3d 4 (2d Cir. 1995); United States v. Somersten, 20 F.Supp.2d 454 (E.D.N.Y. 1998). But see United States v. Crouse, 145 F.3d 786 (6th Cir. 1998) (rejecting departure); United States v. Morken, 133 F.3d 628 (8th Cir. 1998) (same); United States v. Rutana, 18 F.3d 363 (6th Cir 1991) (same), cert. denied, 502 U.S. 907 (1991); United States v. Reilly, 33 F.3d 1396 (3d Cir. 1994) (same).

53. United States v. Stockheimer, 157 F.3d 1082 (7th Cir. 1998) (victims paid $500 for a pad of blank certified money orders which the defendant said could be presented to creditors to pay off debts. The debtors attempted to pay off $80 million in debt, which the district court held as the loss, even though no creditors fell for the transparently bogus scheme. Court of appeals reversed to allow district court to consider departure); United States v. Ensminger, 174 F.3d 1143 (10th Cir. 1999) (rejecting loss enhancement where fraud had no possibility of success).

54. United States v. Brennick, 134 F.3d 10 (1st Cir. 1998).

55. United States v. Lieberman, 971 F.2d

About the Authors

Alan Ellis, a past president of NACDL (1990-1991), is a nationally recognized authority in the fields of plea negotiations, sentencing, appeals, parole and prison matters, habeas corpus 2241 and 2255 petitions and international prisoner transfer treaties. For the past 35 years, He has successfully represented federal criminal defendants and prisoners throughout the United States and abroad. He recently authored several articles on the United States Supreme Court's decision in United States v. Booker entitled All About Booker, Litigating in a Post-Booker World, and Representing the White Collar Client in a Post-Booker World. He writes a regular column on federal sentencing for the ABA's CRIMINAL JUSTICE magazine.

Alan Ellis
910 Irwin St.
San Rafael, CA 94901
415-460-1430
Fax 415-460-1630
www.alanellis.com
E-MAIL aelaw1@aol.com

James H. Feldman is a senior associate in the Ellis firm's Pennsylvania office. Since joining the firm in 1989, he has handled numerous sentencings, appeals, and Section 2255 motions in federal courts throughout the United States. He is the editor of FEDERAL PRESENTENCE AND POST CONVICTION NEWS, and co-author of the FEDERAL SENTENCING GUIDEBOOK and the FEDERAL POST CONVICTION GUIDEBOOK. Mr. Feldman has also authored numerous articles on federal sentencing and post-conviction remedies including Litigating in a Post-Booker World, Representing the White Collar Client in a Post-Booker World, and A 2255 and 2241 Primer.

James H. Feldman, Jr.
Law Offices of Alan Ellis, P.C.
50 Rittenhouse Place
Ardmore, PA 19003
610-658-2255
Fax 610-649-8362
E-MAIL aelaw2@aol.com

LITIGATING
IN A POST-BOOKER WORLD
By Alan Ellis, Karen L. Landau, and James H. Feldman, Jr.

On January 12, 2005, the Supreme Court announced its much-anticipated opinion in *United States v. Booker,* 543 U.S. __, 125 S. Ct. 738 (2005). This article explains the case, its probable effect on federal sentencing practice, and suggests potential areas for litigation in a post-*Booker* sentencing environment.

Booker is the latest in a series of cases that began with *Apprendi v. New Jersey*, 530 U.S. 466 (2000). The *Apprendi* decision held that any fact (other than the fact of a prior conviction) that affects the statutory maximum sentence must be charged in the indictment and then proven to a jury beyond a reasonable doubt. The Court grounded this ruling on the Fifth Amendment's Due Process Clause, which requires that every element in a criminal offense be proven beyond a reasonable doubt, and the Sixth Amendment, which gives defendants the right to have juries make that determination.

Apprendi decided whether a judge could increase a defendant's sentence above the statutory maximum, based on supplemental facts found by the judge at sentencing—not that the tops of correctly calculated guideline ranges were also "statutory maximums." (530 U.S. at 484-89.) After the Court's 2000 decision, every one of the federal courts of appeals held that *Apprendi* did not apply to determinations made under the U.S. Federal Sentencing Guidelines. (*See, e.g., United States v. Casas*, 356 F.3d 104, 128 (1st Cir. 2004); *United States v. Parmelee*, 319 F.3d 583, 592 (3d Cir. 2003); *United States v. Ochoa*, 311 F.3d 1133, 1134-35 (9th Cir. 2002).)

The correctness of these circuit opinions came into question when the Supreme Court decided *Ring v. Arizona*, 536 U.S. 584 (2002). *Ring* involved an Arizona death penalty statute that in some ways worked like the federal sentencing guidelines. In *Ring*, the Supreme Court held that the Arizona death penalty statute violated the principle it had established in *Apprendi*. Arizona law precluded a judge from imposing the death penalty in a capital case unless he or she found certain aggravating factors, over and above the facts found by the jury. That procedure violated the Sixth Amendment, even though the judge had to make his or her finding using a standard of beyond a reasonable doubt. The Court ruled that to be constitutional, the aggravating factors used to increase the penalty from a maximum of life imprisonment to death had to be charged in the indictment and proved to the jury beyond a reasonable doubt. Despite the *Ring* ruling, no federal cir-

cuit revisited its conclusion that the federal sentencing guidelines were exempt from the principle established in *Apprendi*.

On June 24, 2004, the Supreme Court issued its decision in *Blakely v. Washington*, 542 U.S. __, 124 S. Ct. 2531 (2004). *Blakely* arose out of a Washington State sentencing appeal in which the defendant had pleaded guilty to kidnapping. The Washington state legislature, much like the U.S. Congress, had enacted a Sentencing Reform Act that provided determinate sentencing guideline ranges for each offense. Although one Washington statute provided for a 10-year maximum for kidnapping, the Sentencing Reform Act provided for a sentence of from 49 to 53 months based solely on the facts that Blakely had admitted as part of his guilty plea.

The *Blakely* decision clarified the definition of what constitutes a statutory maximum sentence for purposes of applying the *Apprendi* principle. The Supreme Court ruled that the statutory maximum was not the 10 years designated generally for second-degree felonies. Rather, it was ". . . the maximum (the judge) may impose without any additional findings. When a judge inflicts punishments that the jury's verdict alone does not allow, the jury has not found all the facts . . . and the judge exceeds his proper authority. (124 S. Ct. at 2537.) Thus, the statutory maximum was the 53 months established in the sentencing guideline presumptively applicable based upon the defendant's guilty plea.

The *Blakely* decision resulted in a flood of litigation over the federal sentencing guidelines. The circuits split over whether *Blakely* rendered the sentencing guidelines, or the Sentencing Reform Act, unconstitutional in whole or in part. (*Compare United States v. Ameline*, 376 F.3d 967 (9th Cir. 2004), with *United States v. Pineiro*, 377 F.3d 464 (5th Cir. 2004).)

The government separately petitioned the Supreme Court for certiorari in two cases that held that the *Blakely* decision rendered the implementation of the federal sentencing guidelines unconstitutional. (*See United States v. Booker*, 375 F.3d 508 (7th Cir. 2004), *cert. granted*, 04-104, and *United States v. Fanfan*, *cert. granted while pending in the 1st Circuit*, 04-105.)

The *Booker* decision

In *United States v. Booker*, 543 U.S. ___, 125 S. Ct. 738 (2005), five Supreme Court Justices concluded that the Sentencing Reform Act was unconstitutional to the extent that it mandated that a judge increase a defendant's sentence above the statutory maximum, which was either inherent in the jury's verdict, the defendant's plea of guilty, or in admissions made by the defendant. The five Justices reiterated that a defendant's sentence was limited by the Fifth and Sixth Amendments to facts "reflected in the jury verdict or admitted by the defendant." (*Booker*, 125 S. Ct. at 749 (quoting *Blakely*, 124 S. Ct. at 2537.) The Court acknowledged that if the federal sentencing guidelines could be read merely as advisory provisions, their use would not implicate the Sixth Amendment. However, the guidelines were by law not merely advisory, but mandatory and binding, despite the availability of departures in specified circumstances. (*Id.* at 750-52.)

The Justices parted company, however, on the remedy for the constitutional violation that occurred in the *Booker* case. Justice Breyer wrote Part II of the Court's opinion, which set forth the remedy for the constitutional flaw identified in the first part of the opinion. (*See* 125 S. Ct. at 756.) Justice Ginsburg joined the four Justices who dissented as to Part I of the Court's opinion. The Court concluded that to apply the jury trial requirement to the sentencing decisions previously governed by the guidelines would thoroughly contradict Congress's intent in enacting the Sentencing Reform Act and the guidelines, and would be too difficult to administer. (125 S. Ct. at 761-64.) Instead, the Court adopted a remedy that it believed to be closer to its view of congressional intent by employing a severability analysis. (*Id.* at 764-68.) On this basis, the Court excised two provisions of the Sentencing Reform Act that the Court deemed incompatible with the constitutional holding. These provisions, 18 U.S.C. § 3553(b)(1) and 18 U.S.C. § 3742(e), mandated a sentence within the federal sentencing guidelines, and set forth the standards of review on appeal, including a de novo standard of review for any departures. (*Id.* at 764-66.)

Alan Ellis, *a past president of the NACDL, is the founding partner of the Law Offices of Alan Ellis, with offices in San Rafael, California, and Ardmore, Pennsylvania. The firm specializes in federal sentencing, Bureau of Prison matters, direct appeals, and postconviction remedies. He is the publisher of* The Federal Prison Guidebook, The Federal Sentencing Guidebook, *and* The Federal Post Conviction Guidebook, *and is a contributing editor to* Criminal Justice *magazine.* **Karen L. Landau,** *a specialist in appellate and postconviction criminal practice, formerly served as the senior criminal motions attorney to the U.S. Court of Appeals for the Ninth Circuit. She is a member of the Criminal Justice Act appellate panels for the Central, Eastern, and Northern Districts of California.* **James H. Feldman, Jr.,** *is an associate in the Pennsylvania office and handles sentencings, appeals, and section 2255 motions in courts nationwide. He serves as editor of* Federal Sentencing and Postconviction News.

The end result of the *Booker* decision is that the federal sentencing process is governed by 18 U.S.C. § 3553(a). Under that law, the sentencing guidelines have only an advisory function. Because the guidelines are advisory, a district judge must consider the guidelines, along with all other relevant information, in imposing an individualized sentence, *see* 18 U.S.C. § 3553(a) (listing the factors to be considered in imposing sentence), but need not impose a sentence within the guideline range, even if there are no grounds to depart. The Court did not preclude district courts from imposing sentences based on facts that were neither inherent in the jury's verdict nor admitted by the defendant. Instead, because the guidelines are now advisory, they no longer create a "statutory maximum" under *Apprendi* and *Blakely*. Instead, the statutory maximum is the term set forth in the United States Code section that either establishes the offense of conviction or establishes the penalty for a particular offense. There is no constitutional impediment to a sentence anywhere within the statutory maximum.

Booker's impact on defendants not yet sentenced

The immediate effect of *Booker* is profound. Although the Supreme Court expressly directed district courts to consider the guidelines in imposing sentence, the courts are not bound by the guidelines. Rather, the courts are bound by 18 U.S.C. § 3553(a). Under 18 U.S.C. § 3553(a), the key requirement is that the sentence in each case must be "sufficient, but not greater than necessary" to,

> (A) reflect the seriousness of the offense, to promote respect for the law, and to provide just punishment for the offense;
> (B) afford adequate deterrence to criminal conduct;
> (C) protect the public from further crimes of the defendant; and
> (D) provide the defendant with needed educational or vocational training, medical care, or other correctional treatment in the most effective manner.
> (18 U.S.C. § 3553(a)(2).)

Further, the court must consider the kinds of sentences available, 18 U.S.C. § 3553(a)(3); the need to avoid unwarranted sentence disparities among defendants with similar records who have been found guilty of similar conduct, 18 U.S.C. § 3553(a)(6); and the need to provide restitution to any victims of the offense, 18 U.S.C. § (a)(7).

Section 3553(a)(1) also bears on the sentence to be imposed; that section directs the court to consider the nature and circumstances of the offense and the history and characteristics of the defendant. The history and characteristics of the offender include matters beyond a defendant's criminal history, and encompass matters excluded from the court's consideration by the sentencing guidelines. For example, guideline policy statements largely precluded consideration of a defendant's history of childhood abuse, lack of youthful guidance, or drug addiction. (*See, e.g.,* U.S.S.G. § 5H1.1 (discouraging consideration of age); § 5H1.2 (discouraging consideration of education and vocational skills); § 5H1.3 (discouraging consideration of mental and emotional condition); § 5H1.4 (discouraging consideration of physical condition, including drug or alcohol dependence); § 5H1.5 (discouraging consideration of employment record); § 5H1.6 (discouraging consideration of family ties and responsibilities); § 5H1.11 (discouraging consideration of civic and military contributions); and § 5H1.12 (discouraging consideration of lack of guidance as a youth). Those policy statements are no longer binding on district courts. Rather, 18 U.S.C. § 3662 provides that "no limitation shall be placed on the information concerning the background, character, and conduct of a person convicted of an offense which a court . . . may receive and consider for the purpose of imposing an appropriate sentence." This directive might conflict with the guidelines, which in most cases offer only prison. For example, in some cases, a defendant's education, treatment, or medical needs may be better served by a sentence that permits the offender to remain in the community. Thus, a court may impose a sentence outside the guideline range based on factors precluded from consideration by the guidelines. (*See United States v. Ranum*, 353 F. Supp. 2d 984 (E.D. Wis. 2005).)

In cases in which a defendant's history and character are positive, or where the defendant's history contains significant mitigating factors, such as a chaotic and neglectful childhood, an appropriate sentence may be one outside the guideline range.

Another immediate effect of the *Booker* decision is that it is no longer appropriate to speak of the judge granting a "departure" from the guidelines. (*But see United States v. Wilson*, 355 F. Supp. 2d 1269 (D. Utah 2005) (ruling that judges must calculate the traditional guideline range, decide whether to depart from that range, and then, decide whether a variance from the guidelines is appropriate).) The departure methodology was based on the notion that the district courts retained a limited amount of discretion to sentence outside of the guidelines, provided that either the defendant or the government could establish that the case fell "outside the heartland" of the guidelines. (*Koon v. United* States, 518 U.S. 81, 95-96 (1996).) Departures either were based on a ground that had not been taken into account by the Sentencing Commission, or had been identified as a basis for departure by the commission. Since the guidelines themselves are advisory, it is no longer appropriate to

refer to departures. Rather, the advocate should seek a sentence outside the established guideline range.

Courts are likely to continue to calculate a defendant's guideline range the way they did before *Blakely*. Judges will determine the offense level using the application principles established by the federal sentencing guidelines. As before, they will select the offense guideline based on the offense of conviction and will make other guideline decisions using the relevant conduct principles. While there are good arguments on due process grounds for applying a higher standard, *see United States v. Ameline*, 2005 WL 359711 (9th Cir. Feb. 10, 2005) (*reh'g en banc granted*, argued March 24, 2005), courts might still make factual determinations using the preponderance of the evidence standard. They may even continue to talk of "departures." On the other hand, because the guidelines are now advisory, there are fewer impediments to a sentence outside the established guideline range. As in preguideline sentencing, other factors may be more important than the guidelines.

The possibilities for creative sentencing practice abound. For example, in crack cocaine cases, the federal guidelines treat one gram of crack as equivalent to 100 grams of powder cocaine. A judge who, upon considering "the nature of the offense," does not think that crack cocaine is 100 times worse than powder may impose a lower sentence than the guidelines recommend, even though such a disagreement would not have supported a "downward departure" under the guidelines—at least so long as the judge does not go below a statutory mandatory minimum sentence. (*See United States v. Smith*, CR 02-163 (E.D. Wis. March 2, 2005) (reducing sentence for substantial assistance and for disparity between crack and powder cocaine).)

The *Ranum* decision, recently authored by Judge Lynn Adelman, is a fine example of the type of result that can be obtained after *Booker*. There, the judge concluded that a sentence below the sentencing guidelines was justified, because the defendant did not commit the offense for personal gain. In sentencing the defendant to one year and a day in custody instead of the 37 to 46 months called for by the guidelines, the court also considered his positive history and character, his health, and his family circumstances, which included an elderly father suffering from Alzheimer's disease. (*Id.*) Another judge recently imposed a sentence outside the guidelines in a case involving a defendant with a lengthy history of mental illness, whose need for treatment was best addressed by a split sentence in Zone C. (*United States v. Jones*, 352 F. Supp. 2d 22 (D. Me. 2005); *see also United States v. Nellum*, 2005 WL 300073 (N.D. Ind. Feb. 3, 2005); *United States v. Galvez-Barrios*, 355 F. Supp. 2d 958 (E. D. Wis. 2005); *United States v. Kelley*, 355 F. Supp. 2d 1031 (D. Neb. 2005).)

A third judge has explained why *Booker* is not an invitation to "unmoored decision making, but to the type of careful analysis of the evidence that *should* be considered when depriving a person of his or her liberty." (*United States v. Myers*, 353 F. Supp. 2d 1026 (S.D. Iowa 2005).) In imposing sentence, Judge Pratt considered the defendant's history and character, including his moral standards, his service as a role model for his children, the severe negative impact that the felony conviction alone would have on the defendant, the fact that he presented no danger to the community, and his undergoing significant alcohol treatment. After considering all of these factors, the judge sentenced the defendant to probation, rather than the term of imprisonment called for by the guidelines.

However, soon after the Supreme Court announced *Booker*, one judge concluded that the advisory guidelines are entitled to virtually controlling weight. In *United States v. Wilson*, 350 F. Supp. 2d 910 (D. Utah 2005), Judge Cassell gave short shrift to the nonguideline factors set forth in section 3553(a), other than the defendant's criminal history. The court concluded that the guidelines were entitled to controlling consideration largely because of the need for just punishment. The court noted that Congress believed guideline sentences to constitute just punishment and relied on the provisions of the Feeney Amendment, which attempted to limit sentences outside the guidelines. The court also relied on information indicating that public opinion regarding what constituted a "just sentence" for a given crime was close to the sentences prescribed by the guidelines.

Booker and plea agreements

How *Booker* affects defendants who have pled guilty under a pre-*Booker* plea agreement, but who have not yet been sentenced, depends on the particular language of each plea agreement. To the extent that a defendant admitted the existence of certain facts, those facts may be used to determine the defendant's sentence. (*See United States v. Parsons*, 396 F.3d 1015, 1017-18 (8th Cir. 2005).) However, at least in nonbinding agreements under Rule 11(e)(1)(B), stipulations to guideline ranges are not binding on the judge, and would likely not preclude the defendant from seeking a sentence outside the guidelines. On the other hand, the fact of the *Booker* decision does not provide a basis to withdraw a guilty plea on the ground that it was involuntary. (*United States v. Sahlin*, 399 F.3d 27 (1st Cir. 2005).)

Imposition of longer sentences

Theoretically, the *Booker* decision, to the extent that it permits imposition of "reasonable sentences" outside the guideline range, may sometimes permit district judges to impose even longer sentences on criminal defendants. After all, the rules restraining the court from imposing upward departures have been removed, just as have the

restraints on downward departures. This is certainly a risk for defendants who committed their crimes after the date the *Booker* decision was issued.

There also is a risk of a longer sentence for a defendant who appeals, seeking resentencing. The Due Process Clause may protect against this result for those defendants who committed their crimes before January 12, 2005. Because *Booker* in effect rewrote an important aspect of the Sentencing Reform Act, defendants may be protected from a longer sentence, either initially or on remand, by the due process principle precluding retroactive application of a new, adverse judicial interpretation of a statute. (*See Marks v. United States*, 423 U.S. 188 (1977).) This due process principle operates similarly to the Constitution's Ex Post Facto Clause that protects against adverse retroactive legislation. (*See Garner v. Jones*, 529 U.S. 244 (2000); *Miller v. Florida*, 482 U.S. 423 (1987).)

Defendants who are being resentenced on remand also may be protected by *North Carolina v. Pearce*, 395 U.S. 711 (1969), and cases interpreting *Pearce*, which prevent courts from imposing higher sentences at resentencing after a successful appeal, unless the appearance of vindictiveness is eliminated.

Plea negotiation after *Booker*

Booker will certainly affect plea negotiation. Since locking in offense levels will no longer guarantee a sentence within a particular range, counsel will want to think about whether it is better to be free to argue for a much lower sentence or to ensure in a particular sentence with a Rule 11(c)(1)(C) plea. Locking in a sentence may be particularly attractive where there is a greater than average possibility that a court would exercise its discretion to impose a sentence *higher* than the guideline range.

It also is likely that counsel for the government may begin seeking additional defense waivers. For example, government counsel may seek a plea agreement under which the defense agrees not to seek a sentence below the guideline range based on a list of factors. Whether the rules of an open plea warrant entering into such agreements will have to be carefully considered in each case.

Cases pending on appeal

Booker applies to all cases not yet final on direct appeal. If defense counsel did not raise a *Booker*-type objection in the district court, then the court of appeals will review for "plain error." (*United States v. Cotton*, 535 U.S. 625 (2002).) Several federal circuit courts have issued published opinions applying plain error review to *Booker* error. In *United States v. Hughes*, 396 F.3d 374 (4th Cir. 2005), *reh'g granted and op. amended & reissued* 2005 WL 628224 (Mar. 16, 2005), the Fourth Circuit vacated a mandatory guideline sentence as plain error. The

"Litigating in a Post-*Booker* World" by Alan Ellis, Karen L. Landau, and James H. Feldman, Jr., published in Criminal Justice, Volume 20, No.1, Spring 2005 © 2005 by the American Bar Association. Reproduced by permission. All rights reserved. This information or any portion thereof may not be copied or disseminated in any form or by any means or stored in an electronic database or retrieval system without the express written consent of the American Bar Association.

vacated sentence exceeded that which could have been imposed based solely on the jury verdict, but the sentence was properly calculated under the formerly mandatory sentencing guidelines. The Sixth Circuit has issued multiple decisions, largely in accord with the Fourth. (E.g., *United States v. Milan*, 398 F.3d 445 (6th Cir. 2005); *United States v. McDaniel*, 398 F.3d 540 (6th Cir. 2005) (reversing and remanding sentence for *Booker* error under the Armed Career Criminal Act); *see also United States v. Coffey*, 395 F.3d 856 (8th Cir. 2005).)

In contrast, the Eleventh Circuit has applied plain error review in the strictest fashion. (*United States v. Rodriguez*, 2005 WL 272952 (11th Cir. Feb. 4, 2005).) Most recently, that court affirmed a guideline sentence of life imprisonment as "reasonable," even though it increased the defendant's sentence based on conduct of which he had been acquitted. (*United States v. Duncan*, 2005 WL 428414 (11th Cir. Feb. 24, 2005).) The court concluded that while the defendant could satisfy the first two factors of the four-part plain error test, he could not show that the error had affected his substantial rights, because he did "not point to anything indicating a 'reasonable probability of a different result if the guidelines had been applied in an advisory instead of binding fashion.' " (*See also United States v. Antonakopoulos*, 399 F.3d 68 (1st Cir. 2005) (rejecting automatic plain error rule either for Fifth or Sixth Amendment violation or mandatory guideline sentencing).)

The Second Circuit has adopted a slightly different practice, not of remanding cases to the district court for resentencing, but of remanding for consideration whether to resentence the defendant. (*United States v. Crosby*, 397 F.3d 103 (2d Cir. 2005); *cf. United States v. Paladino*, 2005 WL 435430 (7th Cir. Feb. 25, 2005) (providing for limited remand to inquire of district judge whether he would have imposed the same sentence under an advisory guideline regime; if not, court will grant a full remand for resentencing).)

Thus, practitioners should not treat vacatur and remand for resentencing as if it were a sure thing. The *Booker* opinion seemed to contemplate that at least some sentences would be affirmed as neither plainly erroneous, nor "unreasonable." It can be argued that any sentence, whether correctly calculated under the guidelines or not, should be vacated as plainly erroneous because, at a minimum, the district court imposed that sentence under the mistaken impression that the guidelines were mandatory. (*See Hughes*, 396 F.3d at 381 & n.8; *cf. Duncan*, 2005 WL 428414).) Only if the original record admits of no reasonable doubt that the post-*Booker* sentence would be the same could a "plain error" affirmance be appropriate. (*See Cotton*, 535 U.S. at 633; *but compare United States v. Parsons*, *supra*, 396 F.3d at 1017-18 (rejecting remand for resentencing under *Booker* even though district court

had declined to depart downward from the formerly mandatory guidelines, where, pursuant to a plea agreement, the defendant agreed to certain guideline adjustments) and *Duncan* with *Milan*).)

Defendants sentenced after the issuance of the *Booker* decision will still be able to appeal sentences as provided in 18 U.S.C. § 3742(a). However, the sentences will not necessarily be reversed when a district court imposes a sentence outside the properly calculated guideline range. The courts of appeals will review such sentences and underlying section 3553(a) determination for "reasonableness." This standard, while vague, is similar to that which formerly governed appeals of the extent of departures. Defendants will retain the ability to appeal legal errors made in guideline calculation, if the sentence imposed depended on that calculation. Defendants also will retain the ability to appeal procedural errors committed in the imposition of sentence, such as violations of Federal Rule of Criminal Procedure 32.

Another aspect of *Booker* also is being evaluated by the circuit courts: whether a general waiver of the right to appeal the sentence includes waiver of an argument under *Blakely v. Washington*, or *Booker*. The Eleventh Circuit has held that a pre-*Booker* waiver of the right to appeal is binding on the defendant as to a claim based on *Blakely v. Washington* and *Booker v. United States*. (*See United States v. Rubbo*, 396 F.3d 1330 (11th Cir. 2005); *United States v. Grinard-Henry*, 399 F.3d 1294 (11th Cir. 2005).) The Eighth Circuit has reviewed a case for *Booker* error on direct appeal, even though the defendant's plea agreement contained a waiver of his right to appeal. (*United States v. Killgo*, 397 F.3d 628 (8th Cir. 2005); *see also*, *United States v. Jeronimo*, No. 03-30394, slip op. (9th Cir. Feb. 24, 2005).)

Retroactivity on collateral attack

The retroactivity question is a difficult one. Fundamentally, if the rule announced in *Booker* is considered to be a "new rule" of constitutional procedure, then it is unlikely to be retroactive to cases on collateral attack. (*See Stringer v. Black*, 503 U.S. 222, 227 (1992) ("a case decided after a petitioner's conviction and sentence became final may not be the predicate for federal habeas corpus relief unless the decision was dictated by precedent existing when the judgment in question became final.") New rules of constitutional procedure cannot normally be raised in section 2255 motions. (*See Teague v. Lane*, 489 U.S. 288 (1989).) There are some strong indications that *Booker* will not be retroactive to cases on collateral attack.

Teague provides two exceptions to its general rule of nonretroactivity. The first exception applies when the new rule places "certain kinds of primary, private individual conduct beyond the power of the criminal law-making authority to proscribe." (489 U.S. at 307.) That exception would not apply to *Booker*. The second *Teague* exception applies if the new rule represents a "watershed" change that is necessary to the fundamental fairness of the criminal proceeding and improves the accuracy of the criminal process.

The Supreme Court has been reluctant to conclude that new rules of constitutional procedure are so necessary to fundamental fairness that they must be applied on collateral attack. The most recent example of this is the Court's decision in *Schriro v. Summerlin*, 124 S. Ct. 2519 (2004), in which the Court held that its 2002 decision in *Ring v. Arizona* was not retroactive to cases on collateral attack—not even to those cases in which the identical claim had been raised and rejected previously. The *Ring* case involved factual findings beyond a reasonable doubt being made by a judge, rather than a jury. In *Schriro*, the Court concluded that having the findings made by a jury, rather than by a judge, did not itself necessarily improve the accuracy of the criminal process.

There is an argument that the principles underlying *Booker* meet the test for the second *Teague* exception. *Booker* invalidated the mandatory aspect of the guidelines, because when the guidelines were mandatory, *judges* made decisions that affected the "statutory maximum" sentence using a preponderance of the evidence standard, even though the Constitution demanded proof beyond a reasonable doubt in such a mandatory system. Since courts made such decisions using a less fair and accurate standard of proof, it is arguable that the rule in *Booker* was necessary to the fundamental fairness of the sentencing phase of the criminal proceeding and improves the accuracy of the criminal process. (*See United States v. Siegelbaum*, CV-04-1380 (D. Or. Jan. 2005) (stating that at least in some cases, *Booker* may be retroactive on collateral attack).)

In addition, it may be worth noting that the Supreme Court devised the *Teague* rule, in part, to minimize federal court interference with state criminal proceedings through habeas corpus cases. That concern does not apply in section 2255 cases, which involve only *federal* convictions. It is therefore possible that the Court will apply the *Teague* rule less stringently in section 2255 cases than it has in state prisoners' habeas cases under 28 U.S.C. § 2254.

There is a viable argument that the rule announced in *Booker v. United States* that was presaged by *Blakely v. Washington* is not a "new rule"—at least as to a defendant whose conviction was not yet final on appeal when the Supreme Court issued its decision in *Apprendi*, or possibly its decision in *Ring v. Arizona*. If the decision is not a "new rule," then it is not subject to the *Teague* bar. In other words, if the *Booker* decision was "dictated by" the new rule announced in *Apprendi v. New Jersey* as explicated in *Ring v. Arizona*, 536 U.S. 584 (2002), then it is not a

"new rule" subject to the *Teague* bar. (*See Blakely v. Washington*, 124 S. Ct. at 2536.)

A case announces a new constitutional rule if the court bases its decision in the Constitution and the rule was not dictated or compelled by precedent. (*Beard v. Banks*, 124 S. Ct. 2504, 2511-13 (2004).) A decision not "dictated by precedent" is, by definition "new." *Booker* includes a dissenting opinion by Justice Breyer, which was joined by three other Justices, that argues that the result in *Booker* was *not* dictated by *Apprendi* or *Blakely*. This by itself may mean that *Booker* establishes a "new" rule. If it does, then defendants whose cases became final before *Booker*, will not be able to raise a *Booker* issue in a section 2255 motion—unless one of the exceptions to the *Teague* rule applies.

Recently, the Sixth and Seventh Circuits concluded that *Booker*, too, is a new rule, which cannot be given retrospective application under *Teague*. (*Humphress v. United States*, 398 F.3d 855, (6th Cir. 2005); *McReynolds v. United States*, 397 F.3d 479 (7th Cir. 2005).) But the Sixth and Seventh Circuits' conclusions are questionable, given that the *Blakely* decision itself stated that it was an obvious application of *Apprendi*. (*Id.* at 2536.) Indeed, Justice Scalia wrote in *Blakely*: "Our precedents make clear, however, that the 'statutory maximum' for *Apprendi* purposes is the maximum sentence that a judge may impose *solely on the basis of the facts reflected in the jury verdict or admitted by the defendant*." (*Blakely*, 124 S. Ct. at 2537.) Justice Scalia, and the four Justices who joined his *Blakely* opinion, do not appear to believe that *Blakely*, and by extension *Booker*, created a "new rule." The conclusion is even more questionable as applied to *Booker*, which clearly was a direct application of *Blakely*.

Thus, even though the majority in *Booker* apparently believed that the decision in that case was compelled by its previous decisions in *Blakely* and *Apprendi*, courts may well conclude that the rule in *Booker* is not "new."

Similarly, if the rule is not procedural, but rather substantive, then it is retroactive to cases that were final on direct appeal when the *Booker* decision issued. It can be argued that the transformation of the guidelines into an advisory system works a substantive alteration in federal sentencing law in terms of the sentence outside the guidelines. The *Booker* decision also may be substantive, because it does not just affect sentencing procedure, but the actual sentence that can be imposed. If the result had been reversed, meaning, if the guidelines had been transformed from an advisory system to a mandatory one, such a change clearly would be substantive and retroactive application would be precluded by the Ex Post Facto Clause to the extent that it disadvantaged the defendant. (*See United States v. Chea*, 231 F.3d 531, 536-37 (9th Cir. 2000) (later guideline that limited discretion to impose a lesser sentence could not be imposed retroactively); *Mickens-Thomas v. Vaughn*, 321 F.3d 374, 384-85 (3d Cir. 2003) (alteration in parole rules to place emphasis on public safety disadvantaged the defendant; retroactive application violated the Ex Post Facto Clause.)

Does *Booker* affect statute of limitations for 2255 motions?

Section 2255 motions must be filed within one year of the latest of several events. All defendants may file section 2255 motions within one year of the date that a defendant's judgment of conviction becomes "final." If that date has already passed, defendants also have one year from "the date on which the right asserted was initially recognized by the Supreme Court, if that right has been newly recognized by the Supreme Court and made retroactively applicable to cases on collateral review. (28 U.S.C. § 2255.) In this case, the *right* that was "newly recognized" was not necessarily recognized by *Booker*. Courts may find that it was first recognized by the Supreme Court in *Blakely* or *Ring,* or even *Apprendi*. *Booker* simply applied that "right" to the U.S. Sentencing Guidelines. That would mean that defendants whose judgment of conviction became final more than a year ago, may have until June 24, 2005 (a year from the date that *Blakely* was decided), for example, to file their first motions. More than a year has already passed since the announcement of the decisions in *Apprendi* and *Ring*.

Booker and second or successive 2255 motions

Defendants cannot file second or successive section 2255 motions without first getting permission from the court of appeals. There are two bases on which the court of appeals can give permission to file a second section 2255 motion. The first is that there is new evidence that the defendant is innocent (evidence that would not have allowed any reasonable jury to have found him or her guilty). The second is a new rule of constitutional law that the Supreme Court itself has made retroactively applicable to cases on collateral review. (*See Tyler v. Cain*, 533 U.S. 656, 667 (2001).) Although the rule announced in *Apprendi/Ring/Blakely/Booker* is arguably a new rule of constitutional law, so far the Supreme Court has not made it retroactively applicable to cases on collateral review (such as section 2255 motions). Until and unless it does so, defendants will not be able to get permission to file a second or successive section 2255 motion to raise a *Booker* issue. (*See In re Dean*, 375 F.3d 1287, 1290-91 (11th Cir. 2004).)

Conclusion

The *Booker* decision presents federal sentencing advocates with a tremendous opportunity to litigate for fair and just sentences for their clients. Attorneys who have practiced solely under the restrictive regime of the sentencing guidelines must now start thinking in terms of mitigation, alternatives to incarceration, and how to identify a sentence that is "not longer than necessary" to achieve the statutory goals of 18 U.S.C. § 3553(a)(2). Federal criminal defense lawyers may need to take a lesson from their comrades in the realm of capital litigation: these attorneys have repeatedly demonstrated how to save clients' lives through conducting a thorough investigation into the client's social and psychological history and producing evidence that mitigates the crimes committed.■

Inside Baseball:
Interview with Former Federal Probation Officer

Thehe author interviewed Tess Lopez, a former U.S. probation officer for the Northern District of California in San Francisco. For 13 years, she specialized in presentence investigations. In 2005, she took her expertise in the area of sentencing to the private sector and is now a mitigation specialist with a national practice. Contact her at tesslo2@yahoo.com.

Ellis: *As a former probation officer, how do you think probation officers (POs) have responded to the* Booker *decision?*
Lopez: Well, unfortunately, I am not seeing that the presentence reports (PSR) have changed significantly even though the sentencing guidelines are only one of seven factors the court is now required to consider in imposing a sentence. In order for POs to determine which 18 U.S.C. § 3553(a) factors apply, they need to conduct four-hour interviews with offenders and another four to six hours of interviews with family members and close friends to gain this insight. Obviously, that is not going to happen in the current environment of insufficient staff and high caseloads.

Ellis: *How would the probation officers obtain this information?*
Lopez: The defense community, as a whole, needs to change its approach to sentencing. When pro-

bation officers receive a case, they are bombarded with information from the government, including graphic photos of child pornography, pictures of bank robbers, automatic weapons, drugs, and victim impact statements detailing how the offender has robbed good ol' granny of her life savings. The victim may add that your client should rot in jail in the worst of conditions. Such information is presented by the government to the PO in a nice little package complete with a letter outlining its version of the case, its guideline calculations, and an invitation to meet with the FBI agent or case agent to further "enlighten" the PO. Defense counsel usually just calls the PO to schedule the presentence interview and mails the probation form completed by your client providing basic background information.

Ellis: *What can the defense community do differently?*
Lopez: They cannot simply act like "business as usual." The court is not going to receive the information needed to consider sentences outside the guideline range or "variances" from the probation officer, and certainly not from the government. Defense counsel needs to either spend sufficient time with the client and his (or her) family or friends, getting to know him/her so that that the attorney can identify which 3553(a) factors may support a sentence outside the guideline range, or hire a sentencing mitigation specialist to obtain and analyze this information. The lawyer should obtain this information as early in the process as possible so that it is immediately available to present to the probation officer when he or she receives the case and prior to the probation interview. This would provide the probation officer with a more balanced view of the case and presents a preview of the 3553(a) factors that you have identified for consideration.

Ellis: *What else can defense lawyers do to assist the PO in understanding clients?*
Lopez: Provide verification of everything. If your client has an alcohol problem, if not documented by prior arrests, document it, get him or her evaluated, and have family members or friends comment about it. Could the client be abusing alcohol to "self-medicate" and relieve an underlying mental health prob-

Alan Ellis, past president of the NACDL, is a nationally recognized authority in the fields of plea negotiations, sentencing, appeals, parole and prison matters, habeas corpus 2241 and 2255 petitions, and international prisoner transfer treaties with offices in San Rafael, California, Ardmore, Pennsylvania, and Hong Kong, China. He is the coauthor with J. Michael Henderson, of *The 2005-06 Federal Prison Guidebook* and a contributing editor to *Criminal Justice* magazine. Contact him at aelaw1@alanellis.com or go to www.alanellis.com.

em? If your client has significant medical issues, document it and provide a list of medications as well as your client's limitations. If there is a mental health issue, or even if you suspect it's possible, obtain a psychological evaluation. Gather as much information as possible to help the PO, and ultimately the judge, understand who your client is and what led him/her to commit the offense.

Ellis: *Can you provide an example of how such detailed information can support a sentence outside the guideline range?*

Lopez: I'll give you two. 1) Historically, lack of guidance as a youth and unfortunate childhood experiences were not relevant in determining whether a sentence outside the guideline range was appropriate. It was called a "prohibited factor." I could never understand this "logic." Repeated studies have shown that a disadvantaged youth is a root cause of crime in this country. At last, post-*Booker*, this information must be considered by the court as it relates to the personal history or characteristics of the defendant. 2) As you often say, Alan, "If you think your client is crazy, guess what? He may be crazy. Have him/her evaluated by a mental health professional." I second the motion. If your client has suffered significant abuse or trauma, these experiences may have contributed to his/her pattern of making poor decisions or engaging in risky, unacceptable behavior. Defense counsel may be able to show that the childhood experiences were extreme and contributed to the client's participation in the offense. Perhaps the client recently commenced counseling and can demonstrate new insight about wrongful conduct. These unfortunate childhood circumstances and the client's motivation to address his/her behavior may convince the court that a lower sentence is warranted.

Ellis: *In your experience, do many clients have mental health issues?*

Lopez: To illustrate an example: In a white collar case, the client is an exceptionally bright, high-functioning, and very successful individual. By all appearances, he is very skilled, highly motivated, and works 18-20-hour days, landing promotions and executive privileges. Where is the mental health issue here? A little digging and a psychological evaluation reveals that the client is an obsessive-compulsive perfectionist who suffers from depression and anxiety. The overwhelming desire to be successful personally and financially may cause an ordinarily law-abiding person to "cross the line" into inappropriate or illegal behavior. The exceptionally bright, successful client is later diagnosed with bipolar disorder. Studies have shown that many people silently and unknowingly suffer from mental illeness. The Justice Department estimates that half of America's prison and jail inmates have symptoms of mental health problems. However, the latest statistics by the U.S. Sentencing Commission (2002) reflect that only 2.6 percent of inmates received downward departures for diminished capacity (U.S.S.G. § 5K2.13). If half of the inmates have symptoms of mental health problems, yet only 2.6 percent are receiving departures, are the judges simply insensitive? Or, does the problem lie at the feet of defense counsel who are not taking the time to conduct a thorough investigation into the client's social and psychological history? Unfortunately, I believe it is the latter.

> On first contact, ask for the dictation deadline.

Ellis: *How can defense lawyers make sure the court gets the detailed information?*

Lopez: Unfortunately, it is often too late to wait and simply respond to the draft presentence report. When the lawyer first makes contact with the probation officer, ask for the "dictation deadline" or date that the draft PSR is due to the supervisor. Make sure all information regarding the client's background is provided by that date. As experienced federal practitioners well know, it is often difficult to convince a PO to make significant changes to the report once it is disclosed. However, if the information is simply not available until after the draft report is disclosed, the lawyer who responds to the draft PSR should request that the PO include the more detailed information into each section of the PSR. Defense counsel may even email a detailed report to the probation officer so he/she can cut and paste the information into the report. Finally, outline each factor that you want the PO to consider under parts E (factors that may warrant a departure) and F (factors that may warrant a sentence below the guideline range under 18 U.S.C. § 3553(a)) of the PSR and make strong arguments to support these requests.

Ellis: *Why not skip the process and just put everything in the sentencing memo to the court?*

Lopez: Two reasons: First, judges continue to rely on probation officers during sentencing and some judges are significantly influenced by the probation officer's opinion. If the PO is receptive to a variance it may be key to convincing the court to consider a sentence below the guideline range.

Second, in the event that your client receives a prison sentence, the only documentation received by the Bureau of Prisons (BOP) about your client is the PSR. This information (or lack of information) will dictate whether the client is sent to a dormitory-style camp or, at the very worst, a maximum security prison. For example, if your client has a pending state case and no disposition is noted, the BOP may treat the open case as a detainer. As a result, clients may be scored higher, be precluded from participation in programs that could benefit them and reduce their sentences, and affect whether or not they are sent to a more secure facility with fewer privileges.

Ellis: *How can lawyers address a pending state matter that may result in a detainer?*

Lopez: Defense counsel should schedule a court date to have the previous matter disposed and then alert the judge that the matter is pending disposition. Request that the sentencing go forward and notify the judge that you will provide a certified copy of disposition. Request that the judge order the probation officer to modify the PSR to include the disposition (before sending the PSR to the BOP) once the PO receives this documentation. Also request that the judge's clerk wait to release the judgment and commitment order (J&C) until this happens since the issuance of the judgment triggers the BOP designation process. Having the client sentenced on the prior offense *after* sentencing prevents the client from having another scorable conviction. Requesting that the PO be directed to change the previously pending matter to one that has been disposed of eliminates the issue of having a pending matter or "detainer" for BOP designation purposes.

Ellis: *Is there anything else defense counsel can do to get their point across to the probation officer?*

Lopez: Yes, in cases in which the client is convicted by a jury or enters a plea without a written plea agreement, the parties have not agreed on guideline calculations or departures. Often, the parties have opposing views on loss figures, guideline calculations, ex post facto issues, criminal history, and departures. I recommend that defense counsel present their entire view of the case in a straightforward letter to the PO as soon as possible. More importantly, I strongly recommend that defense counsel request to meet with the probation officer to discuss their position on these issues. This is particularly important in a complex case involving numerous counts, various ways to calculate the guidelines, which guideline is appropriate, which guideline book is appropriate, etc. Personal contact with the probation officer builds rapport and offers an opportunity to explain your position. Sometimes a case is so complex that the PO would welcome the opportunity for defense counsel to explain their version of the case. Remember, the PO wasn't present at trial. A personal meeting also assures the lawyer that the PO understands the case and his or her position. Generally speaking, when working with the probation officer, a little extra effort goes a long way.

Ellis: *Is it your impression that the judges are responding to the* Booker *decision and the* Booker *remedy by treating the guidelines as just one of seven factors and are sentencing outside the guideline range?*

Lopez: Unfortunately, the data indicate that federal sentences are not lower post-*Booker*. Once again, it is up to the defense bar to bring about change through creative advocacy. As noted by Karen L. Landau, whom I know is "of counsel" to your firm, in an article she coauthored with you and your senior associate, James H. Feldman, Jr., "Litigating in a Post-*Booker* World" (CRIM. JUST., Spring 2005, at 24.), "federal criminal defense lawyers may need to take a lesson from their comrades in the realm of capital litigation: these attorneys have repeatedly demonstrated how to save clients' lives through conducting a thorough investigation into the client's social and psychological history and producing evidence that mitigates the crimes committed."

I think it is easier for a judge who was on the bench in the preguideline days to welcome the wiggle room and lack of structure than it is for those judges whose only experience has been with guideline sentencing. It will take time for the defense community to appreciate the importance of operating differently and more thoroughly and it's going to take time for some judges who like the structure of the guidelines to adapt to the change, as it "goes against their grain." But you and your colleagues can help them do so. ∎

Tips on Getting Your Client Into the Best Prison and Released at the Earliest Opportunity

By Alan Ellis

At sentencing, most defense attorneys rightly focus on guideline objections, departures, and variances. They want to make sure not only that the sentencing guideline range comes out as low as possible, but also that the court is persuaded by any arguments for a sentence below the bottom of that range. While working for the lowest possible sentence is the defense attorney's most important job, defense counsel should not overlook ways to ensure that the client gets into the best possible prison and is released at the earliest opportunity.

Although it is the policy of the Bureau of Prisons (BOP) to place an individual in the least restrictive facility within 500 miles of the inmate's "release residence" for which he or she qualifies, many inmates end up serving their time far from their families and under harsher conditions than necessary. It doesn't have to be that way. There is a lot a defense attorney can do to ensure that his or her clients do their time in the best possible facilities. First, defense attorneys need to understand how the BOP classifies its facilities, and the characteristics of each type of facility. Second, they need to understand how the BOP decides what type of prison is appropriate for a particular defendant. Finally, defense attorneys need to know what to do to increase the chances that their clients will be sent to the prisons they want. The first step in this process is to download the BOP's Security and Classification Manual (Program Statement 5100.008), which lays out the BOP's rules for security classification scoring. It is available in PDF format from the Bureau's website: www.bop.gov.

Once a defense attorney understands how the system works, there are four things he or she can do to ensure that a client serves time in the best possible facility. First, counsel should ensure the accuracy of the information on which the Bureau will rely to make its designation decision. Second, counsel should score the client and search for Public Safety Factors (PSF) to determine the appropriate security level. PSFs (such as "deportable alien") can preclude camp placement for otherwise qualified defendants. Third, counsel should consult with the client to determine which facility at the appropriately-calculated security level the client prefers and then ask the sentencing judge to recommend that facility to the BOP, as well as to provide reasons in support of that recommendation. Counsel should, of course, suggest reasons as part of his or her request. Finally, counsel should, in appropriate cases, request self-surrender.

The most important thing defense counsel can do to ensure designation to the lowest security prison possible is to make sure that any inaccurate information in the Presentence Investigation Report (PSR) is corrected. The BOP relies almost exclusively on the information contained in the PSR to decide where a defendant will do time – as well as to make other important correctional decisions (such as whether a defendant is eligible for the Bureau's Residential Drug Abuse Program – "RDAP").[1] It is for good reason that the PSR is known as the "bible" by prisoners and BOP staff alike.

If defense counsel objects to inaccurate information at the time of sentencing and the judge sustains those objections, defense counsel must make sure that the PSR is corrected before it is sent to the BOP or, at a minimum, that formal findings are made by the judge pursuant to Fed.R.Crim.P. 32(c)(1) and attached to the PSR before it is forwarded to the Bureau. A finding made in the judgment in a criminal case (preferably in the statement of reasons portion) will also suffice.

For example, if the PSR incorrectly states that your client has a history of aggressive sexual behavior, even when it's not part of the conviction offense, he or she will not go to a federal prison camp despite what the otherwise calculated score might indicate or the judge recommends. Similarly, if the PSR reports that the client has a pending criminal case, the BOP will give the client a higher security level score – even if that case was dismissed prior to sentencing. Inaccuracies like these may result in the client being designated to a higher security prison unless they are objected to and corrected prior to the entry of judgment.

It is also important for counsel to make sure that the PSR's criminal history score is accurate. The addition of one criminal history point may not change a defendant's Criminal History Category ("CHC"). But it can still be important to object to these seemingly harmless additions, and then to appeal if the district court denies the objection. Normally, a criminal history point that does not affect the sentencing range is "harmless error", but not always. In *United States v. Vargas*, 230 F.3d 328 (7th Cir. 2000), the Seventh Circuit remanded for resentencing based on a seemingly inconsequential criminal history point. The Court reasoned that the error was not "harmless," because it "might have affected" the district court's denial of the defendant's motion for downward departure based on the defendant's contention that his criminal history category significantly overrepresented the seriousness of his criminal history.[2] A single point might also affect prison designation, since the BOP now uses criminal history points to calculate an individual's security level.[3] Criminal History Points can affect the type of facility to which the offender may be assigned, even if the judge sentences outside the guideline range.

It is also important for defense counsel to make sure that the PSR adequately documents any drug (illegal as well as prescription) abuse or alcoholism. Many defense lawyers and defendants tend to downplay substance abuse problems, under the mistaken belief that revealing such problems can harm the client. Unless a client's substance abuse problem is adequately documented in the PSR, he or she may not qualify for the Bureau's Residential Drug Abuse Program (RDAP) and will not get the chance to earn up to a one-year reduction in sentence pursuant to 18 U.S.C. § 3621(c)(2), which permits such a reduction for nonviolent inmates who successfully complete a residential drug treatment program in a BOP facility.

Attorneys often try to magnify their client's health problems in hopes of gaining sympathy from the sentencing judge. A focus on mental or physical problems can be warranted if it supports an argument for a lower sentence based either on Guideline Program Statements, such as USSG § 5H1.3 (p.s.) (mental and emotional conditions "not ordinarily relevant") and § 5H1.4 (physical condition "not ordinarily relevant"), or the non-guideline factors 18 U.S.C. § 3553(a) requires a court to "consider." Otherwise, highlighting these problems may have the unintended consequence of the client being designated either to a medical facility rather than a camp, or to a different camp that is not the client's first choice.[4]

This is not to say that medical problems should be minimized. Medical problems should be accurately reported in the PSR. Otherwise, not only may the client not receive appropriate medical treatment and be required to perform physical labor precluded by a medical condition, the client may be designated to a prison that is not equipped to provide the level of care the client needs. It is also important for the PSR to list medications the client has been prescribed.

Initial placement is based on classifications that consider both security and medical needs. The BOP makes these classifications based on information in the PSR. Each defendant is assigned a security level based on offense characteristics, sentence, and history, as well as a Level of Care (I, II, III, or IV) based on his or her anticipated medical requirements. The facility nearest the defendant's legal residence, as reflected in the PSR, that meets the security and medical care level requirements and which has bed space available is generally designated for service of sentence.

Finally, it is important to ensure that the PSR lists the correct client address. Since "release residence" is defined by the BOP as the defendant's legal address that's listed on the PSR, the BOP will attempt to house your client near that address. If that address is not only far from family and friends who want to visit your client, but also far from the area to which you client intends to relocate upon release, you should consider requesting that another address be used.

While it is important for defense counsel to make sure the facts in the PSR support the most favorable designation, it is also important for defense counsel to obtain a judicial recommendation supported by reasons. Unfortunately, some judges don't like to recommend particular places of confinement at sentencing, believing that they are not "correctional experts," or because they have become discouraged by letters they get from the BOP advising them that their recommendations cannot be honored in a particular case. In these situations, counsel should point out two things. First, when the BOP fails to honor a judge's recommendation, it is usually because the judge has recommended a facility incompatible with the defendant's security level. Counsel should assure the judge that the defendant qualifies for the facility requested. Second, counsel should remind the court that, although judicial recommendations are only recommendations, that does not mean they are not important. Not only does 18 U.S.C. § 3621(b)(4)(B) specifically contemplate these recommendations, but BOP Program Statement 5100.08 says that the BOP welcomes a sentencing judge's recommendation and will do what it can to accommodate it. Bureau statistics show that in approximately 85% of the cases in which the defendant qualifies for the institution recommended by the judge, the court's recommendation is honored. However, the BOP has recently stopped writing explanatory letters to judges when recommendations are not followed.

Without a recommendation from the judge, prison overcrowding may prevent your client from being designated to the facility he prefers –

even if he qualifies for it, and even if it is close to his home. Should there be only one slot open at a prison, such as the Federal Prison Camp in Fairton, New Jersey, and there are two defendants who want that placement, the one with the judicial recommendation is more likely to get it. If your judge is reluctant to make recommendations, it may help to get a copy of the Bureau's Program Statement 5100.08 and show the Court the page that deals with judicial recommendations.

Sometimes an unsupported recommendation may not be enough. Before sentencing, draft the language you want the court to use to make the recommendation. For example, if the reason your client wants a particular facility is that it has the RDAP program, the court's recommendation should say that the Court recommends the facility for that reason. If the Court agrees to include the reasons you have suggested, offer to submit your draft to the judge through the courtroom deputy clerk.

Finally, it is important to ensure that if your client is a United States citizen, the citizenship is verified by the U.S. Probation Officer and duly noted as verified in the PSR. This is not generally a problem for persons born in the U.S., but can be especially important for naturalized citizens, because if such citizenship is not verified in the PSR at the time of initial designation by the B.O.P., an individual who might otherwise be eligible for placement in a Minimum security camp will be designated instead to a Low security prison, the next higher security level.

NOTES

1 552 U.S.___, 128 S.Ct. 586 (Dec. 10, 2007).

2 552 U.S.___, 128 S.Ct. 558 (Dec. 10, 2007).

3 For more information on the RDAP program, see Alan Ellis and J. Michael Henderson, "Getting Out Early: BOP Drug Program," Criminal Justice (Summer 2005); and Alan Ellis and J. Michael Henderson, "Reducing Recidivism: The Bureau of Prison's Comprehensive Residential Drug Abuse Program, Champion (July 2006). Both articles can be found at www.alanellis.com.

4 *See* USSG § 4A1.3 (p.s.).

THE LAW OFFICES OF ALAN ELLIS
WHO WE ARE, WHAT WE DO AND HOW WE DO IT

The Law Offices of Alan Ellis is a full-service sentencing and post-conviction law firm representing exclusively federal criminal defendants and inmates throughout the United States and abroad.

For over 39 years, the firm has worked with defendants, inmates and consulted with many of the nation's leading criminal defense attorneys to develop strategies that obtain the lowest possible sentence for clients, to be served at the best facility possible, with the greatest opportunity for early release.

Areas of expertise include:

- Plea negotiations
- Sentencing representation and consultation
- Prison designation, transfers, disciplinary matters
- Rule 35 motions
- Direct appeals in all circuits from conviction and sentence
- Supreme Court practice
- Habeas corpus 2255 and 2241 petitions
- Parole representation
- Prisoner transfer treaty work for foreign inmates, and Americans arrested abroad
- International criminal law

The firm has an international practice with regional offices in Mill Valley (San Francisco) California, Ardmore (Philadelphia) Pennsylvania, and soon to be opended, China. Many of the firm's attorneys have served as federal law clerks, and several are former law school professors. Affiliated with the firm are two sentencing specialists one of whom is a licensed clinical social worker and the other a former federal probation officer, and two federal prison consultants formerly employed by the Bureau of Prisons.

Approximately one half of our work comes to us from defense attorneys requesting our assistance on cases. The remainder of our cases comes to us as a result of defendants, inmates or their family and friends contacting us directly with requests for representation.

With increasing frequency, we are being called upon to consult and assist earlier on in the criminal defense process. This is due in no small part to the importance of plea-bargaining and the significant recognition that planning and preparation for sentencing and post-conviction remedies must not be relegated to the post-verdict or post-plea stage of the proceedings.

While we cannot guarantee or predict a favorable outcome in any particular case, we will not take a case which we believe has no merit. We will only handle a case if we think the client has a reasonable chance of success. Accordingly, when an individual or his family or friends call us, we require a thorough review of the record before we will agree to represent the person.

About the Authors

Alan Ellis, a Past President of the National Association of Criminal Defense Lawyers, is a criminal defense and human rights lawyer with offices in San Francisco, Philadelphia, and Shanghai, China, with 39 years of experience as a practicing lawyer, law professor and federal law clerk. He is a nationally recognized authority in the fields of federal plea negotiations, sentencing, appeals, parole and prison matters, habeas corpus 2241 and 2255 petitions and international criminal law. For the past 39 years, he has successfully represented federal criminal defendants and prisoners throughout the United States and Americans arrested abroad charged with foreign crimes. He is a sought-after lecturer in criminal law education programs and is widely published in the areas of federal sentencing, Bureau of Prisons matters, appeals and other post-conviction remedies, with more than 120 articles and books and 70 lectures, presentations and speaking engagements to his credit.

According to Federal Lawyer Magazine, Alan Ellis is "one of this country's pre-eminent criminal defense lawyers." The San Francisco affiliate of ABC-TV has said that he is "The best in the business." Verdict magazine quotes other legal commentators as saying that he is "the go-to guy in America if you're in deep trouble with the law." The United States Court of Appeals for the Ninth Circuit in a published decision has described him as a "nationally recognized expert in federal criminal sentencing."

Mr. Ellis authors a regular quarterly column on Federal Sentencing for the American Bar Association's *Criminal Justice* Magazine.

Amongst his publications are the highly acclaimed *Federal Prison Guidebook*, the *Federal Sentencing Guidebook* and the *Federal Post Conviction Guidebook*. Mr. Ellis also publishes "*Federal Sentencing and Post Conviction News.*

He has also authored several articles on the United States Supreme Court's decision in *United States v. Booker* entitled "All About Booker," "Litigating in a Post-*Booker* World," and "Representing the White Collar Client in a Post-*Booker* World." With regard to the federal prison system, he has published "Securing a Favorable Prison Placement" and "Reducing Recidivism: The Bureau of Prisons Comprehensive Residential Drug Abuse Program."

In the area of international criminal law, he has recently authored and published "Americans Arrested Abroad," a companion article to his earlier "Going Home: An Introduction to International Prison Transfer Treaties," and in 2007 was awarded a prestigious Fulbright Senior Specialist grant by the U.S. State Department to conduct lectures in China on American criminal law and its consitutional protections. He was the first practicing American criminal defense lawyer to have been invited to the Peoples Republic of China.

Mr. Ellis is

• AV rated by Martindale-Hubbell. An AV Rating is Martindale-Hubbell's highest ratings for attorneys. It shows that a lawyer has reached the height of professional excellence. He or she has usually practiced law for many years, and is recognized for the highest levels of skill and integrity.
• U.S. Department of State Fulbright Award grantee
• Fellow of the American Board of Criminal Lawyers
• Former member of the Board of Directors of the National Council on Crime and Delinquency
• Past President to the ACLU of Central Pennsylvania

At the forefront of critical issues facing the criminal defense bar, Mr. Ellis founded the NACDL Lawyers Assistance Strike Force which has attained national prominence for its support of criminal defense lawyers who are prosecuted, subpoenaed and harassed as a result of their ethical and vigorous defense of their clients. He also founded NACDL's Amicus Curiae Committee which, during his tenure, filed briefs in over 40 major state and federal cases throughout the United States. For his work in founding NACDL's Strike Force and Amicus Committee, he was awarded the Association's 1983 Robert C. Heeney Award for distinguished contributions to the criminal defense bar.

Mr. Ellis has been interviewed extensively by the national media, including the *New York Times, Washington Post, Time Magazine, USA Today*, "NBC Nightly News", "ABC World News Tonight", "CNN Prime News", "CBS Radio News", and "National Public Radio".

He has been featured in the *American Bar Association Journal*, the *San Francisco Recorder*, the *Philadelphia Inquirer*, the *Pacific Sun* and profiled by the syndicated TV magazine show, "In America/The West" as well as KGO TV, the ABC affiliate in San Francisco. Mr. Ellis has written numerous editorials on criminal justice issues which have appeared in the *Wall Street Journal, San Francisco Chronicle, Atlanta Constitution, San Diego Union, Oakland Tribune, Sacramento Bee, St. Louis Post Dispatch, Chicago Tribune, Salt Lake City Tribune, Pittsburgh Press*, and *LaOpinión*.

He has served as a member of the editorial board of the Criminal Practice Manual published by the Bureau of National Affairs Inc.

A former law professor and federal law clerk to two federal judges, Mr. Ellis is a 1967 graduate of Villanova University School of Law and an editor of the Villanova Law Review.

James H. Feldman, Jr., practices federal post-conviction criminal defense out of his Ardmore, Pennsylvania, office, and is of counsel of the Law Offices of Alan Ellis. He has handled numerous sentencings, appeals, and 2255 motions in federal courts throughout the United States, and is Editor of Alan Ellis' Federal Presentence and Post Conviction News, and co-author of the Ellis firm's *Federal Sentencing Guidebook* and its *Federal Post Conviction Guidebook*. Mr. Feldman has also authored numerous articles on federal sentencing and post conviction remedies including Litigating in a Post-*Booker* World, Representing the White Collar Client in a Post-*Booker* World, and A 2255 and 2241 Primer.

After earning his law degree in 1976 from the University of Cincinnati College of Law, Mr. Feldman engaged in the solo practice of law there until 1982, when he moved to Philadelphia to serve as staff attorney for the Central Committee for Conscientious Objectors. As a result of his work with CCCO, Mr. Feldman is one of a handful of attorneys in the United States experienced in litigating habeas petitions on behalf of members of the United States armed forces.